THE PURPOSE OF PAIN

HOW TO TURN TRAGEDY INTO TRIUMPH, BECAUSE LIFE'S NOT SUPPOSED TO SUCK!

JAY NIXON

Dad, I never really knew you, but I'm extremely grateful for you. Our experience has made me the person I am today.

"I learned that courage was not the absence of fear, but the triumph over it."

~ Nelson Mandela, *Long Walk to Freedom*

ISBN: 978-1-942761-95-2

Publishing Services and Book Design by Archangel Ink

CONTENTS

INTRODUCTION

Most five-year-olds don't do well with dates aside from Christmas and their birthdays. But I wasn't most five-year-olds.

June 28, 1980. I remember that day like it was yesterday. It wasn't my birthday, and we were only halfway to Christmas. But it has played a bigger role in my life than nearly any day since.

The sun rode high in the West Texas sky as I stood at the top of a hill close enough to my house that my mom could still see me. The heat was thick, but it wasn't going to stop me from loading rock after rock into my little red wagon. This random day of summer vacation in sweltering West Texas marked the beginning of my own personal hell.

I had started my way down the hill when I saw the Texas Highway Patrol car snaking its way up our long and winding driveway. Even at five I sensed something wasn't right. It wasn't every day that a cruiser rolled up to our house.

I walked in the front door as an innocent and curious little boy trying to figure out what was going on. I didn't know the next time I walked out that door, I would be broken.

I stepped into the house and looked around. My mom was weeping with the crushing sorrow reserved for tragedy.

My dad was dead.

He had not been sick. He was as healthy as a man could be when he left our house, but a head-on car crash took him from us. All my friends grew up with dads to lean on, to learn from, and to toss the football around with. On June 28, 1980, I was robbed of all of that.

I've heard people say, "Pain is not a punishment." That five-year-old boy sure felt punished. I've also heard, "Time heals all wounds." For twenty-five excruciating years, my life personified the contrary. I lived in a whirlwind of pain I thought would never diminish.

As I grew up, that pain affected every area of my life. I never took care of my body or my bank account as a young adult. Why? Because I had a car crash full of evidence telling me that people don't live long enough for sustained health and wealth to be a concern. My relationships were tainted for decades because I lived with a very real fear of losing any people I loved. And although I grew up in a religious Texas town, my spirituality or any connection with a higher power was virtually nonexistent. It's hard to blame a little kid for giving up on God when he loses the guy who means the most to him so abruptly.

The pain that started that hot summer day in 1980 didn't let up for a long time. It was an unrelenting wave of emotional, mental, and physical suffering.

In truth, the suffering I endured didn't need to happen.

My dad died once, but emotionally and mentally I watched him die every waking moment of the years that followed. *Feeling* the pain of such an enormous loss might be expected, but *carrying* the pain with me for decades was on me. I can't blame my dad for that. I can't blame God. I can't blame the Universe. I chose the option of suffering instead of finding a purpose for my pain.

I took one event and allowed it to form the foundation of my story of pain, suffering, and victimhood. I was the kid whose dad died, and I played the role well. I let people feel sorry for me. I felt sorry for myself. I put the baggage of my dad's death on my five-year-old shoulders and lugged it around for most of my life.

At some point, I realized I had the option of putting the baggage down.

This book is about letting go of the pain that weighs you down and discovering the purpose behind what's been hurting you.

Everyone has their brand of pain. It's subjective and depends on your life experiences. There's no competition or ranking system; pain is pain. I don't care if you lost a family member, were bullied as a kid, or got dumped by your high school sweetheart ten years ago. It's all painful. It all hurts.

But what I've learned—and hope to communicate to you through the pages in this book—is that there is hope for you if you're hurting. Pain is not a death sentence.

Pain doesn't have to determine how your life is shaped if you don't want it to. By the end of this book, you will understand two very important things about pain.

First, there is a purpose for your pain. Tony Robbins has said, "Life is not happening to you, it's happening for you."[1] It's the truth. In your moment of pain and despair, you may call "bullshit," but I promise you that Tony's statement is spot on. There is a reason you're experiencing pain. If you can turn your attention toward that reason and embrace it, your life can transform into something unbelievable. On the other side of your pain stands the life you were born to live and love.

Second, pain doesn't have to lead to suffering. Another important quote comes from Haruki Murakami: "Pain is inevitable. Suffering is optional."[2] Since you are a human being, you are bound to experience pain. My father was killed. You may have lost a pregnancy, been fired, or have a strained relationship with your mother-in-law. Pain comes in many forms and flavors, but it will find you no matter how hard you try to live a life of sunshine and rainbows. You don't have to stay in the shadows, though. Suffering is optional. It took me twenty-five years to understand Murakami's truth.

---

1 Tony Robbins (@Tony Robbins), Twitter, November 10, 2016, https://twitter.com/TonyRobbins/status/1127740350557315073 .

2 Haruki Murakami, *What I Talk about when I Talk about Running: A Memoir* (New York: Vintage Books, 2008).

Pain will come, but you can opt out of misery.

Whether you picked up this book because the title spoke to you or because a friend recommended it, I know you've been hurt. Hell, it may not be past tense yet—pain may be your current reality. No matter when you felt it or how it happened, I'm glad you're here. Your pain is likely different from mine, but it hurts just the same.

Death hurts.
Divorce hurts.
Watching your child be bullied hurts.
Recalling when you were bullied hurts.
An athletic dream ended by an injury hurts.
A squandered opportunity hurts.
Watching your bank account rapidly evaporate hurts.
Living a life of hopeless mediocrity hurts.

It all hurts.

This book is about turning hurt into hope and pain into purpose. It's been a while since I decided to put down the baggage my five-year-old self picked up back on June 28, 1980. My life is nothing short of amazing now. I own my own business, I'm crazy about the woman I love, and I get to help people flourish in their health, fitness, and mindsets on a daily basis.

This book is my gift to anyone who is ready to step away from a life of pain. In the following pages, I'm going to show you how to take back ownership of your life. You don't have to run out the clock in a state of misery. I promise.

These mountains that you are carrying, you were only supposed to climb.

~ Najwa Zebian

PART 1

PAIN

CHAPTER 1
PAIN PERSONIFIED: MY STORY

My pain began with the loss of my dad, but it didn't end there. That event was merely the catalyst—the first chapter of my story. I wish it all began and ended with the car crash that took my dad's life and seemingly destroyed mine, but the pain of loss and despair morphed into the repeating theme of my childhood and young adulthood.

While I fought fear, depression, and anger internally, my external world became an all-out war of trauma. Black clouds of emotion followed me around for decades, made worse as I continued to lose people I cared about. I lost my grandfather to emphysema ten years after my dad was taken. This time, as a fifteen-year-old, I was more aware of the loss. As a little kid, I remember asking people when my dad was coming home and when I'd see him again. I didn't really get it. When my grandfather passed, though, I understood; I knew the two most important men in my life were gone before I was within shouting distance of manhood.

Fast-forward to late 1993: Christmas Day to be exact. I never really had what you might call a typical Christmas after losing my dad. While I did my best to embrace the holiday cheer swirling around me, it was hard to play into the joy, happiness, and light of the season with darkness in my heart. One man who did his best to make those dark times a little brighter was our next-door neighbor, Lonnie. He stepped up and filled my fatherless void in whatever capacity he could, at Christmas and throughout the year. On December 25, 1993, my family and I went over to wish Lonnie and his family a Merry Christmas and to exchange some gifts only to be hit with another curse. During our visit, Lonnie had a heart attack. I gave him CPR until the ambulance arrived, and then I watched him ride away, hoping that the EMTs could take care of him. He died later in the evening. Another man I trusted, cared for, and relied on was gone, and I was barely eighteen.

They say that deaths come in threes. Man, I wish I had been so lucky. "Lucky" may not be the word I'm really looking for here, but I would've been grateful for a reprieve from significant losses. Unfortunately, the pain kept coming. When I was twenty-five, just when I thought I could start living my life without being reminded of how brief it can be, my best friend put a shotgun in his mouth and pulled the trigger.

I'm not telling you all of this for shock value. I'm not sharing this with you to get sympathy. I just want to paint a clear picture of the type of pain I've experienced. By the time I was twenty-five years old, I had suffered enough loss to last a lifetime. I thought I was cursed. I thought I was being punished. I struggled mightily to go on living while death kept knocking on my door.

Looking back, the most difficult part for me is remembering how the loss of my dad hardened my five-year-old soul. That kid had no idea how to process the situation. Without a fully developed conscious mind, the only tools I had to operate with were the animal instincts of fear and self-protection. I built mental and emotional walls around myself that grew taller with each tragedy I encountered. I didn't let anyone in because I was scared I might lose them if they got too close. I never came out from behind the wall. I was petrified of what might happen if I opened myself up to the world that had been so cruel to me.

I remained a scared little boy for decades. Fear was my mode of operation. You wouldn't have known it had you met me back then, though. I didn't look scared, at all. I wouldn't allow myself that kind of vulnerability.

Instead, I was a tough guy. I truly believed I needed to become the man of the house at five years old, so a man I became. I felt that showing my emotions was weak. I sensed I needed to be strong. My inability to deal with my sadness and depression left me with anger and rage to spare; anyone who got in my way found out the hard way they had made a mistake. Hurt people hurt other people, and I was hurting like hell.

I was a beast on the football field. In a game where every

play ends with two guys trying to smash each other's heads in, I thrived. It was my place to let my anger and frustration out for the life that had hardened me, and I took full advantage to unleash the pain. Every hit was fueled by the thought, *Why did my dad die before I really knew him?* Every tackle carried the weight of the heavy heart I was unable to open.

I was always in protection mode. I was always scared of losing someone else. My life had presented enough evidence to validate my fear. My state of mind and emotional well-being never evolved from the time my dad passed. My five-year-old self had a firm grip on my mental steering wheel for decades because fear felt safer than the vulnerability of opening up and being hurt or let down. I grew older, but my mentality stayed stuck in the mud.

Isn't that crazy? At ten years of age, I was still a scared little five-year-old. At twenty, I was still a scared little five-year-old. The same remained true as I approached thirty. I wore masks to fit in, but underneath it all I was still a terrified kid carrying his fear and pain with him everywhere he went.

Your story of pain and suffering may star different characters and follow a different plot line, but baggage haunts whoever carries it. It doesn't matter how you got hurt or how long you lugged the hurt around, it will always cause a ripple effect. My story wove its way through every area of my life, staining everything in its path. There's a good chance that whatever hurt you (or is still hurting you) suffocated your relationships, your health, your wealth, or your spirituality as well. Those four categories of my life—relationships, health, wealth, and spirituality—were forever changed by all of the shit I went through between the ages of five and twenty-five. Before I can show you how my pain became my teacher, I first have to show you how my pain took control of these areas of life. The themes you'll see arising in my story are not unique to me; you very well might have lived similar circumstances. Whether you've been in the same trenches or different ones, it's important for us to dig into the darkness of our pain to uncover its purpose.

Without the darkness, there can be no light. To show you how I've successfully moved past my pain, I must allow you to see how terribly I navigated through it.

• • •

Before I let you into my world completely and show you how my pain tore through my life like a tornado, I want to stop and acknowledge something very important: the hopelessness and despair I experienced had less to do with the events than with *what I made those events mean.*

We're all storytellers. We cherry-pick the events and experiences that flow through our lives and create a narrative around them. Without that narrative, everyone's life story would read more like an encyclopedia than a compelling novel. When we observe how our life has played out, we don't want a list of facts, figures, and dates. We want it all to mean something. We want it to have mattered.

A significant problem with this urge to create meaning in our lives, though, is that as humans we live through moments of pain, frustration, and sadness. When we begin telling stories with pain in our hearts, the narrative imprinted on our consciousness comes out a little skewed. The more pain we're holding onto, the farther our story strays from reality. We fill in the blanks with sorrow and sadness and give ourselves reasons to feel like we're trapped by the circumstances of our lives.

I didn't suffer for as long as I did because of my dad's death, my grandfather's death, or any trauma that followed. I suffered because when my dad died in a car accident, I picked up an emotional pen and began writing my story as a scared five-year-old kid. That little boy didn't put the pen down for twenty-five years.

I created stories about how normal death was, how life was far too short to care about anything in a real way, and how God couldn't be real. They were compelling narratives, and I believed them to be true. The only thing I didn't realize was that the tales were written from the perspective of a kid whose life experience was limited to death, destruction, and the pain they leave behind.

The stories I told myself were the reason my pain stayed for the long haul and morphed into suffering. The tales I wrote allowed me to live small, scared, and sad.

Now, I didn't write this story entirely on my own. There were plenty of people who showered me with sympathy, reminding me that I had a right to feel sad. People would tell me it wasn't fair that my dad had been taken from us so early, or how terrible it must've been to watch our family friend Lonnie slip away while I gave him CPR. With each condolence, I would double down on all my reasons to be upset and angry about how my life was playing out.

"That's right! I've really seen some terrible things. I have every right to feel how I feel."

No one had a problem enabling my frustration. But not one brave soul cared enough to tell me what I needed to hear: "Jay, I know you're hurting. You have every right to be frustrated. But you have just as much right to *quit* feeling the way you do."

It's probably not polite to tell a kid as depressed and angry as I was how he might feel. It's much easier to validate the feelings I had because there was plenty of evidence to justify my sadness.

But knowing that I could *choose* something else, a different way of operating, would have been such a gift. The stories I created about my life were so vivid to me that I had no idea they could be changed.

I didn't have to stay sad.

I didn't have to stay angry.

I didn't have to stay frustrated.

I eventually figured out how to wrestle the emotional pen from the hand of my five-year-old self and to begin writing stories that empowered me to change my life. Once I began writing more compelling and inspiring narratives about my life—figuring out what my story meant and how I could use all of my experiences for a greater good—my life changed forever.

My suffering began and ended through the power of story. I created so many that mired me in places I didn't want to be. Then I discovered how powerful our stories really are.

As you read through this book, I invite you think about the stories you've created in your life.

Maybe you watched your parents go through a nasty divorce, and you can't quite figure out why love seems so elusive for you. I'd be willing to bet that a younger version of you wrote a story long ago about how real love doesn't exist and is not worth pursuing.

Maybe your family struggled to get by when you were a kid, and as an adult you find yourself in the same situation. There's a good chance that your eight- or nine-year-old mind created a narrative something like, "Money isn't important" or "You don't need money to be happy." They're not terrible stories to have packed away in your subconscious mind, but it's awfully hard to generate wealth when you keep thinking about how it doesn't matter.

Maybe, like me, you experienced the death of someone close to you when you were young and have had a hell of a time letting people into your life as a result. The only thing keeping you from the closeness you desire is the story you've created about what it means if and when someone earns the right to be part of your world. Will they all die? Well, yes. It comes with the gig of being human. But nobody dies because of you; that's just the story you've let yourself believe.

It doesn't matter what your story is. It really doesn't.

What does matter is that you have the power—and, frankly, the responsibility—to rewrite the narrative. Let me tell you what I so desperately needed to hear back then: You get to choose your story.

You get to decide what everything means to you, how you feel about it, and what you're going to do about it. There is no truth except for the truth you decide to believe.

It took me decades to realize I'd spent years spinning my wheels, believing things that only existed in my mind. Those "facts" kept me in pain. Eventually I started to rewrite my story, which brought me here, to a place where I'm honored to shed light on the purpose that is woven into pain of all shapes and sizes.

But we can't skip to the end of the story; that never does

it justice. The following pages will show you just how much my stories derailed my life. As I look back, some of the answers seem so clear now, but when I was living in them, it wasn't as easy. You may see yourself in some of my stories. If you do, I hope they will allow you to see the falsehoods for yourself and to make the necessary changes.

Remember, your stories can be your greatest gift or your biggest curse. The beautiful part? You have a choice in the matter.

CHAPTER 2
MY HEALTH STORY

My fear? Getting picked for the "skins." If I took my shirt off, my soul would be bared along with my chest. The skinny frame I was born with had been insulated by years and years of emotional eating. I wore my extra weight like a battle scar, the effect of the emotional war I had been losing as a result of the death happening around me. It wasn't just a day on the court with the boys. It felt like emotional torture every time, just hoping I could be a "shirt" instead of a "skin."

Any time I ended up on the skins squad, my heart sank. I was ashamed of what I hid underneath my T-shirt. Years of eating my feelings and hearing my brother call me "fat boy" had me hoping and praying I could keep my shirt on every time we played.

Truth be told, I wasn't even that big. Was I bigger than I needed to be? Yeah, probably. Was I obese? Not at all. But my self-image and self-worth were trending so low at the time that I hated the way I looked and didn't think I deserved anything different. It didn't matter if I was shaking as teams were picked on the basketball court or doing my best to go unnoticed at school, I was petrified of anyone seeing what

I had become.

So why had I let myself get this way? Because I wasn't living my life. I was living inside the story I had created.

My story said people die young, so why not have a handful of cookies when no one's watching?

My story said tragedy is ready to strike at any moment, so what's the point of trying to take care of your body?

My story said anyone I love dies, so—being a human being who feared death on some level—wouldn't it make sense not to love myself?

The story I told myself about my health and my wellness caused me to eat my feelings and then feel terrible about it. I didn't know that each cookie or candy I ate threw my pain out into the world like a boomerang; it left for a brief moment of indulgent bliss but came back tenfold when I looked at myself in the mirror.

I couldn't figure out how to release the pain inside. It's clear now that the path of emotional eating wasn't going to heal me, but back then, I spent many nights digging to the bottom of an ice cream pint trying to see if it would. And then I'd hide behind my clothes so no one could see what I'd become.

I specifically remember one maroon hoodie I had. Now remember, I grew up in Texas, where hoodies are seen about as often as snow on Christmas Day. There was no need for anyone in their right mind to wear a hooded sweatshirt on a regular basis in that kind of heat, but my maroon hoodie was my security blanket. It covered my imperfections and the extra weight I was so ashamed of. Rain or shine, I threw my hoodie on and let it block anyone from seeing the "me" that I had become.

Sweating it out in my security blanket was much easier than taking an honest look at myself and who I was becoming. But something else in Texas gave me a much-needed escape from the pain that my everyday getup personified:

Football.

If you have a pulse and come from where I did, football represents an inevitable part of your life. For me, it became my heavy-hitting heaven.

The gridiron was my safe haven, the one place my pain could run loose and actually benefit me and my teammates. To others, the game may seem violent. To a younger me, it was simply a beautiful way to express my rage. I loved the moment of impact, of transferring all of my sadness and sorrow into the poor guy who was on the receiving end of the hit. Looking back, I feel bad about the pain I may have inflicted on other guys, but I needed a place to transfer all my pain, and football gave it to me.

I thought I had finally found an arena of release, a place I could truly rid myself of all of my pain. For a while, I did just that. The more I played, the healthier my body looked. The more hits I delivered, the more frustration I released.

My coaches loved to say, "Leave it all out on the field." I left more out on the field than anyone I'd ever played with. I came to each game ready to score points and make some tackles, and I left my emotional baggage somewhere between the lines.

Or so I thought.

Around the age of thirteen, it seemed that years of viciously slamming my body into other boys my age had caught up to me. I began to experience aches and pains in my hands and feet, specifically in the small joints. It got worse and worse as the years passed, eventually leading to a diagnosis of arthritis. As much as I wanted to square up and fight the world for all the trauma I had experienced, I couldn't even make a fist to throw the first punch. The arthritis got so bad that I couldn't close my hand, open a jar, or do anything else your average teenager can easily do.

"God, Jay! You can't win!"

Ain't that the truth. Well, let's be clear: that was my truth.

For years I just fought through the pain. The world had hardened me at an early age, so I had mastered the skill of just powering along. I kept playing football and doing everything else I normally would. I wasn't going to let a little pain in my hands and feet stop me.

But the pain had other ideas. Over time it grew into a monster that brought me to my knees. I remember lying in my bed, eyes open and filled with tears. I couldn't sleep due to the pain, and I was fed up with the emotional games life continued to play with me. If there is a hell, I can't imagine it being worse than what I experienced back in those days. By the age of twenty-five, my pain registered as 12 on a 10-point scale.

My experience with arthritis kept fanning the flames of my story of hopelessness, despair, and sorrow. "Of course my body would give up on me. Everything and everybody else has."

First my dad, now my health. I expected it to get worse because that was all I knew. My life was like a tunnel with no light at the end of it. Things kept getting darker with each step forward.

Until they didn't.

• • •

Today a game of shirts versus skins wouldn't faze me at all. Not because I'm in love with the way I look—let's be honest, that chubby kid from West Texas still lives inside my head, and sometimes I still see myself through his eyes. The difference is now I know that all the judgment I feared was coming from me and not from anyone watching. I know now that everyone on the court was dealing with their own stuff and didn't have the time or desire to take on my insecurities too.

These days I own and operate Thrive Fitness Studio in Palm Desert, California. Every morning I look out at my clients and see a sea of irony. One of the areas where I had the least control in the first half of my life—health and wellness—has become the vehicle through which I serve my purpose here on this planet. Every day I wake up and give people the opportunity to take their health back into their own hands.

Speaking of hands, my arthritis has all but gone away. What used to register at a 12 on a 10-point scale now hovers around a 2. The condition that used to plague me all night has up and left. I sleep like a baby, snoozing the night away with a smile on my face and fulfillment in my heart.

So what shifted? How did my story change?

I'd had enough. I reached a point when I knew that the path I was walking would destroy me in the end. I made a decision: I was ready for a BIG shift. Here's the thing—I didn't even know yet what I needed, I just knew I needed a change. Sometimes transformation in your life can start with the smallest of intentions.

I looked at my situation and realized I had more to do with it than I understood. I used to blame sneaking cookies and the extra weight I carried around on all the terrible stuff that had happened to me. I used to blame my arthritis on football. And I thought my life was cursed. But somewhere along the line, I chose to take a little more responsibility.

It wasn't the cookies' fault that my waistline grew over time. It was my belief that I deserved them because of the trauma I'd experienced. I thought life was short anyway, so who cares if I eat the whole sleeve of Oreos.

It wasn't football's fault I could barely get out of bed in the morning. My physical pain was simply an expression of my mental and emotional agony. The longer I bottled up how I felt, the more the suffering showed up in my joints. The more I tried to hide my emotional scars, the more pain seared through my body. Since I was too scared to take a look at my internal wreckage, I never let any of it go. With each new traumatic event, I just stacked more terrible news atop of an overflowing emotional garbage can.

When I woke up to the fact that no one was going to empty the garbage can but me, I understood I had to get my hands dirty and see what I'd let pile up for all of those years. The first thing I did was take a hard look at what I perceived to have happened to me and observe the circumstances through the lens of what I had created in my life.

For a very long time, I saw my physique and my arthritis as two things that had fallen into my lap. I'd say, "I got chubby," or "I got arthritis." I made it seem like I was in the wrong place at the wrong time and received those things without having any say in it. I challenged myself to flip that notion on its head and see my circumstances as things I made happen. Instead of blaming my bad luck, I started blaming myself. Not in a self-loathing, "You're a terrible person" kind of way. I just took more ownership than I ever had. Instead of being an observer of a story I thought I had no control over, I became the writer and narrator. From that point on, it was my narrative to create and mine to adjust.

I told myself that if I'd had something to do with the deterioration of my body, then I had the power to reverse it. I looked back at the way I had operated as I'd created my ailments and experimented with doing the opposite to see what happened.

Instead of blaming everyone else, I began to blame myself (compassionately). Instead of believing things could only get worse, I became optimistic about how things could and would get better. (Side note: at the time, I wasn't all that confident in this new belief, but it was better than the alternative I had been living.)

Instead of hating myself for letting my circumstances wear me down, I began loving myself for surviving through it all and making the decision to enact some changes.

Instead of staying closed off and not letting anyone into my shitstorm of emotional baggage, I opened up to people and became vulnerable for the first time in my life.

And it was scary as hell. But it changed everything.

I started to eat better and to hit the gym more consistently, creating more and more healthy habits along the way. Losing the emotional weight made way for quite the physical transformation.

My arthritis went from keeping me up at night to not bothering me at all. I never took any pain meds or prescriptions for it along the way. As I got rid of my emotional pain, there was nothing left to express itself in the form of arthritis. I'm human, and with that, I am imperfect. There are days when the pain flares up, but the more I lubricate my mindset and emotions, the less my arthritis comes out to play.

I am the healthiest I have ever been. Twenty years ago, I would've assumed I'd be dead or in a wheelchair by now. But today I run around my fitness studio like a madman, hyping my clients up to bring out the best in them. I'm relatively pain-free and move around better than nearly everyone my age.

I just needed a new story to tell about my pain. Once I figured out how to take more responsibility for it, everything fell into place.

CHAPTER 3

MY WEALTH STORY

The same story that kept me from honoring my body kept me from respecting my bank account. Why should I care about building wealth if I wouldn't be around to enjoy it?

If you want to thrive in the area of wealth, committing to a long-term vision and showing up consistently for the sake of that vision is essential. Unless you win the lottery or are gifted a fat check through an inheritance, making money and building a career you can take pride in requires time. The money often has to marinate as you master your craft and figure out what works and what doesn't.

For most people, a long-term vision makes sense. If the assumption is you're going to live for a while, having a general game plan while you're alive and kicking is a reasonable exercise. But for me, a guy who watched people pass on well before their time was up, a long-term vision seemed more like a fairy tale. I genuinely assumed I wouldn't be here long enough for money or work to matter. People like to say that life is short, but I really believed my time was severely limited. I didn't think I would live to see the day I would be rich or have a career I enjoyed, so the effort needed didn't seem worth my time. I was just winging it until my number was called, which I assumed could be any day.

My mentality for most of my childhood and early adulthood was one of survival. I was just trying to live to see another day, month, or year. Most twenty-somethings were dreaming big about what they wanted to create in the next thirty years. I was just hoping I got to live thirty years, period. All I had was the twenty-four hours in front of me.

You might think that living for each day and not worrying about what the future has in store is a healthy perspective. In some cases, it absolutely can be. When someone uses that frame of mind to be present and productive in each moment, it can be super helpful. But I wasn't present within each moment; I was petrified. I was scared I was on a shot clock much shorter than everyone else's. So what was the point of saving, investing, or being smart about my cash flow?

I racked up $40K in credit card debt. I didn't think I'd ever have to deal with paying it back, so I spent money like a trust-fund baby on spring break. I lived paycheck to paycheck no matter how much money I made. If I made more money, I'd dump it into something else I didn't need. I figured I could ride out my lifestyle until it was my turn to go.

It wasn't just this mindset that contributed to the way I treated money. There was a subtle undertone that made an already bad situation much worse: my lack of self-worth. My self-worth was hit hard by the pain of my dad's death.

Without my dad around to help put food on the table, I witnessed my mom and the rest of my family struggle to make ends meet, both emotionally and monetarily. It didn't seem like any of my friends at school or in my neighborhood were going through what I was, so I just assumed I didn't deserve to have the life they did. I figured if I was meant to be happy and loved, I would be. If I was worthy of all the stuff I wanted, I would get it.

My bank account was one of the most popular places for my low self-worth to rear its ugly head. A subconscious voice whispered, "I don't deserve to have money or nice things." It was like a record playing on repeat for fifteen years. This belief wasn't a conscious one; it was baked into my soul, and I had no idea.

I'd get a new job, get a raise, or come into some money, and still find myself in debt. Truth be told, I worked my ass off but still found money elusive. Most people see their careers as a marathon, playing the long game and conserving their energy for the long haul. But not me. I went all out 100% of the time because I thought I had less time to live than everyone else. And still, money never stayed with me long. Cash started burning a hole in my pocket as soon as I received it. At the conscious level, I was betting on a short life span, not thinking about long-term savings. On a subconscious level, though, there was a piece of me that kept rejecting anything above my level of self-worth. Since my experiences—and what I made those experiences mean—had set my self-worth bar so low, it didn't take much for me to sabotage my way back to $0.00.

I had so many wants and desires in my adulthood, but no matter how much hard work and tenacity I brought to the table, all of those accomplishments eluded me.

Until they didn't.

• • •

My fingers dance across the keys this morning as I sit on my back patio watching the sun rise over our home in southern California. I look to my left and see the palm trees surrounding our house, and I smile. The sun sparkles off the water in the pool and Jacuzzi in the center of our backyard. Over the steam from my fresh cup of coffee, I see the statue of Buddha just beyond our tranquil pool of water. I feel like Dorothy: "We're not in Kansas anymore." I have come a long way from the days of spinning my wheels, scraping by, and hoping for my big breakthrough of cash flow.

So what happened? Did I win the lottery? Did I inherit a lump sum of cash?

Not at all. In fact, I'm glad I didn't. If I had been given a big bag of money, I would've found a way to spend it. No, I began to see the story I've described in this chapter for what it was: fictional.

What I thought was a hard and fast law—everyone I love dies before their time—was really just the exception. Probability says that you and I are going to live for a long time, and once I shifted my thoughts and realized I had a lot of life left, I allowed myself to start thinking bigger, bolder, and brighter. I allowed myself to dream about my career and what I could create within it. With this new ambition as the wind beneath my wings, I started down the path to becoming the owner of Thrive Fitness Studio.

These days when I work with my clients at Thrive Fitness Studio, I like to repeat one of my favorite sayings: "You will never get more out of life than you believe you deserve." When I speak it into their lives, I'm letting them know they will never have the body and health they want until they do the inner work and decide they are worthy of them. I coach them from the inside out, as I explain in my book *The Overweight Mind*, building up their mindset so they can keep the progress they create during a workout.

I always understood those words on a conceptual level. It makes sense that you can only acquire (and keep) what you think you're allowed to have. But my experiences with money in early adulthood really shifted this idea from an Instagram-worthy quote to a deep-seated belief.

I believed I wasn't worthy of all of the nice and shiny things I said I wanted. Even though I desired them on a conscious level, my subconscious patterns of low self-worth caused me to sabotage my efforts. But you know what? They call it self-worth for a reason. Once I realized my worth was decided by me and not by other people or circumstances, I pulled myself out of the hole I was living in. By empowering myself to believe that I deserved what I desired—and telling myself this new story over and over again—I began to bring my dreams into reality.

I can't say this enough: what you tell yourself about yourself will create the experience around you. Your story can make or break you. If your bank account is looking empty or your career is draining your soul, reexamine your story about what you think you deserve. Because you will never get more out of life than you believe you deserve. The metrics you measure your wealth and prosperity with are simply physical expressions of what you've decided you deserve.

Want more? Decide that you're worthy of it.

CHAPTER 4
MY RELATIONSHIPS STORY

Back in my football days, every once in a while my coaches would try to motivate us with the phrase, "Play to win! Don't play not to lose!" As a kid, I didn't understand. The more I thought about it, the more it confused me. If we played to win and were successful in that mission, we were victorious. If we played not to lose and were successful in that endeavor, we were still victorious. Either way, we won. So why did they keep shouting it at us?

Now that I've lived a little and gotten just a touch wiser, those motivational quips make a little more sense to me. Playing to win versus playing not to lose is more about energy and intention than anything else.

When you play to win, you are going all out. You leave it all on the field—you don't even consider the thought of losing. When you play to win, you are more present in each play, and you compete with the confidence that victory is the only possible result. When you decide to play to win, you play fearlessly.

When you play not to lose, however, you focus more on what could go wrong than on all the things that could go right. Rather than going all out, you're hesitant and unsure. When you play not to lose, the only confidence and certainty you have is that the other team could easily win the game if you make one mistake. When you bring the wrong kind of energy to the table, you're just trying to survive until the final whistle, hoping that nothing goes wrong along the way. When you play not to lose, you play with fear.

Now, I know you didn't pick up this book looking for cliché football jargon, so let me get to my point.

For a very long time after my dad died, I approached every relationship with a protective, terrified, "not to lose" energy. Rather than loving all out and trusting that it wouldn't be taken away, love scared me. So, rather than giving people my all, I was hesitant and lacked confidence. I just hoped whatever love I experienced wasn't going to up and leave me.

I loved my dad, and when he was taken from us, it crushed me. It hurt so damn bad. And since my brain had hardly developed any form of rationality, I put the following pieces together:

I loved my dad. My dad died.

Therefore, people that I love die. If someone is close to me, they will surely die as well. It's best to keep my distance and just hope no one else I care about dies as a result of knowing me.

From that point on, I spent a lot of years just trying not to lose anyone else. Rather than loving people fully and fearlessly, I kept my distance, hoping my arm's-length approach would keep them safe. In my mind, the last person I said "I love you" to wasn't breathing anymore, so I couldn't risk letting those words leave my lips again. In fact, the one person desperately needing to hear me say it more than anyone else didn't get the privilege for a very, very long time. My poor, grief-stricken mom probably would've given anything to hear her little boy say, "I love you, Mama," but I just couldn't bring myself to do it. I went years without telling her that I cared about her. It's not that I didn't, but I was petrified of what might happen if I let her in on my little secret. The concept of love and the meaning I had attached to it kept me quiet and distant with my mom and anyone else I knew. I loved them all, but I did not tell them.

Pretty messed up, right? You can imagine how such a dysfunctional story affected my relationships as I grew older and "developed" my love-life theory. As a young adult, I'd go out looking for love and find a way to lose it every time it answered my call. I'd meet a girl, enjoy her company, and smile, thinking, "Things might be turning around for me. I think I might be able to do this love thing, after all." But somehow, someway, things would fall apart as quickly as they had come together. I was a master of self-sabotage. I either dated girls that weren't a good fit for me or wrecked the relationships with ladies who were exactly what I needed.

In my conscious mind, all I wanted was something to fill

the void of the love I missed in my childhood. But in my subconscious, my self-worth was still running on empty. Whether it was finances or females, as soon as I felt I was reaching the threshold of what I deserved, I would find a way to get rid of it. For the life of me, I couldn't hold on to the love I so desperately desired.

My inability to connect with other human beings didn't just manifest in my romantic pursuits, either. You'd think that after losing our dad, my brother and I would have had each other's backs and taken care of one another. I mean, who else could truly empathize with my situation better than him? Even with our stories so closely aligned, we acted like enemies back then. We beat the hell out of each other whenever we could, to the point that my mom couldn't leave us alone. God forbid we'd give our mom a break from all the stress and sadness she'd been carrying. Instead, we just kept at each other's throats for years on end.

I had friends. I had family. I had girlfriends. But I never felt connected to them. I wanted to be close, but I just couldn't get there. I would not allow it. More importantly, I was terrified of being open and vulnerable. I knew if I let people in on my pain, my anger, and my fear, they would know the real me (and they would not like what they found).

That was my greatest fear of all. There was a lot of darkness inside I didn't want anyone to discover. There was a lot of pain I was too scared to face. My soul needed to heal, but the thought of sharing my story, my feelings, and my thoughts about my experiences made me want to curl up in a ball and die.

I was surrounded by people, but I felt alone.

Until I didn't.

• • •

At a certain point, playing defense and keeping people at a distance became exhausting. The little five-year-old who was still running the show had grown tired of pushing people away, putting on a brave face, and letting people think everything was okay. Things were *not* okay, and I was dog-tired of trying to pretend.

It didn't happen all at once, but I began to let my guard down, slowly but surely. Was it scary as hell? Absolutely. But I know I wouldn't be where I am today had I not faced that fear. I confided in people I figured I could trust, pulling back the curtain to reveal the turmoil raging within. What happened next was amazing.

For decades, I imagined if I showed anyone my inner wounds, they would leave my life as quickly as my dad did. I thought if I opened up and got vulnerable, the people I trusted with the information wouldn't like what they saw.

I was wrong.

Instead of running away, they held on tight. They didn't

judge or offer up empty platitudes. They showed compassion and empathy, giving me the confidence to release the inner tension that had knotted me up for so long. They helped me see that what happened to me wasn't my fault, no matter how much I tried to convince them otherwise.

They showed me that, despite all the terrible things I'd seen and experienced, my life was still worth living. As my mindset began to change, I realized the fault in the story I had believed for so long. The fear I associated with being vulnerable and sharing my inner world came from the idea that if I opened up, I would feel even lonelier. I thought if people knew the real me, they would disappear. But when I began to give a select few people the inside scoop, I realized that being vulnerable and giving them access to my heart and soul was the key to creating the connections I so desperately wanted.

This shift in my story was huge. And it's the one I believe will help you most. If you've ever found yourself keeping people at a distance, scared to let them in on the secrets you've kept under wraps, my advice is to do the one thing that probably scares you the most: open up. Let them in. Tell them how you really feel and show them who you really are.

The thing is, if you can't give them the real you, it's impossible to create an authentic connection. If you're not showing them your genuine self, your relationships—romantic or not—will be as fake as the facade you parade around behind.

We human beings are an interpersonal species; we thrive on meaningful connection with each other. If you keep yourself closed off for too long, the loneliness will eat away at you. I've heard that loneliness can be as dangerous for your health as smoking fifteen cigarettes a day. I think we can all agree that smoking like a chimney isn't beneficial to your health, so if the above is true, it would follow that we should feel just as strongly about eradicating the lack of connection in our lives. True, meaningful relationships are the juice of life. But you won't ever get to enjoy a deep level of connection if you're unwilling to bring the real you to the table.

You may be afraid of showing the world the scars you've accumulated, but those scars won't heal in seclusion. Physical wounds need oxygen to heal, and your emotional wounds are no different. You have to let them breathe. When you open up to the people around you, the world has a way of opening itself up to you.

But you have to go first—fearlessly. It's so worth it, though. Trust me.

CHAPTER 5

MY SPIRITUALITY STORY

There can't be a God. There's just no way. If there were, why did my dad have to die before I really knew him? If there were, why did my life go from bad to worse year after year? Isn't God supposed to help you? Isn't God supposed to have your back?

I never felt like I had anyone in my corner, let alone an all-knowing and all-powerful God, so I came to the conclusions above over and over again. I had a deck full of trump cards against any claim about how gracious, giving, and loving God supposedly was.

Them: "God's got your back."

Me: "Then why did He let my dad die when I was five?"

Them: "It's all part of His plan. Trust that God will heal your wounds and help resolve your pain."

Me: "Really? Because all I've known since then is death, destruction, and suffering."

Them: Open mouth; insert foot

I didn't want to hear any of it. Mind you, the five-year-old inside of me was still holding the pen, crafting my story of death and despair, and the ripple effect it had on all parts of my life. The spirituality and religion story line was short and to the point. It was more of a headline, really: God doesn't exist.

Before my dad died in the car accident, I honestly don't recall going to church or learning about God. From most of the science I've read, the pre-five-year-old brain is pretty much mush when it comes to memory anyway. Go ahead and try to dig deep for your earliest recollections. Odds are you won't find one before your fifth birthday. But for me, my dad's death flipped a switch in my brain. It turned the lights on, so to speak. The memories of my life began on that day in 1980.

In the wake of his passing, I remember being thrust into the church. As you can imagine, West Texas had quite the buffet of options when it came to praising a higher power. There were more churches than you could shake a stick at. Sundays are about church and football where I come from, and with my family desperately trying to fill the void that my dad left behind, the Sunday service was our place to attempt to find some peace.

For many people, the church is a place of community, a place of belonging. You head to the church and catch up with people in your neighborhood, sharing blessings and struggles. In many ways, church is a safe space for people to be supported and feel the love. It represents a larger version of family to them.

But I didn't get those vibes on any of the countless Sundays I spent sitting in a church pew. I felt like an outsider in the Lord's house. The preacher would stand in front of us, telling story after story about how much God loved us and was there to watch over us as we walked through life. The people around me would nod their heads in agreement, praising God, Jesus, and anyone else they believed to be taking care of them. I just kept thinking, "I must be missing something. How could the big guy be real if my dad's gone, my mom's depressed, and everything around me is going down in flames?" I felt like everyone else who came to church was part of some exclusive club of blessings and miracles, one that wouldn't let me in.

Even though I felt like I didn't belong, I still kept showing up. I *wanted* God to be real. I *wanted* Him to heal all the pain I had in my heart and soul. I'd go to church, say my prayers, and beg for answers. To be honest, I wanted to believe in God more than anyone in any church I attended. I needed it all to make sense. I needed to know that I wasn't being punished. I needed to understand the reason for my suffering.

I kept asking questions, but I never got any answers. I concluded that either God hated me or He just wasn't real. Since believing the latter would cause me less pain—I couldn't face believing God didn't love me—I lost all hope in the existence of a higher power. It was easier for me. If God wasn't real, that took the edge off of my dad's death a bit. If I believed there was a God and he had still let my dad die, the resulting sense of betrayal hurt like hell. But if I believed He wasn't real at all—that there wasn't some big guy up in the clouds who could've saved my dad and chose not to—it hurt a little less.

As I committed to the thought of no God, I still felt conflicted. I wanted to believe there was a reason my mom, my brother, and I went through what we did. I wanted some all-powerful being to come down and save us. Hell, I also wanted someone to blame for all the tragedy and destruction I'd witnessed. Without a God, none of this pain had a purpose, and I had no one to accuse.

That inner conflict stayed with me for a very long time. I wrestled with spirituality and religion for years. A part of me hated the whole idea of it, while an equal part of me wanted some sort of saving grace. I spent years sitting on the spiritual fence, waiting for clarity to strike me.

And then it did.

• • •

My viewpoint of life, the events within it, and the stories I created to give my circumstances some sort of meaning changed when I came across the following phrase:

Life doesn't happen to you; it happens for you.[3]

I heard that line at a time when I was not only ready to hear it but also prepared to listen to the message within the words. I was in my early thirties and starting to unravel the false stories I'd created about my life. I had begun opening up to people, building trust, working on my self-worth, and taking responsibility for my thoughts and actions. I was ever so slightly shifting the tide in my life, but I couldn't quite find a way out of my piss-poor relationship with God, the Universe, or whatever label you'd like to use for a higher power.

And then those words swooped in and smacked me upside the head. I had spent my entire life pissed off about how many things had happened *to* me. I had never considered—or never wanted to consider—the idea that maybe all of it happened *for* me. The words gave me the opportunity to look at my past through a different lens.

Maybe my dad died so I could learn how to be strong.

Maybe I got arthritis so I could see how much my inner pain reflected outward, and then use the knowledge to help others.

Maybe I made money, lost money, found and quit jobs so

3 Tony Robbins, Unleash The Power Within, SAP Center, San Jose, CA, November 10-13, 2016.

I could figure out with certainty what I wanted to do with my life.

Maybe I watched life leave the eyes of our family friend Lonnie so I could appreciate the days I had left.

Maybe I kept my distance from the girls I dated in early adulthood because I needed to wait until I found the woman who was my perfect match.

Maybe all of my pain had a purpose. Maybe it all came with lessons that were mine to learn.

Life doesn't happen to you; it happens for you. The more I went down the rabbit hole opened by those words, the more I believed they might be true. And if my life was happening for me, that would mean someone (or something) had it planned out for me. I wouldn't say I had a "come to Jesus" moment or anything, but I began to have faith in *something* out there. I began to believe in a force of energy bigger than myself. I started to trust that my life had meaning again.

And even with all the pain I'd endured, I slowly felt it start to wash away. My pain started to have a purpose. I began seeing it all meant something. I did not know what, but I understood I was meant for more than the struggle I had endured for decades.

I was connected to something. I still don't know what the "something" is. But I know this book wouldn't be in your hand had I not found a new story to tell about my spirituality. Without that connection, I'd still be stuck. Instead, I'm honored to help you find your pain's purpose and to guide you as you discover how you can climb to new heights in your life.

PART 2

PROGRESS

CHAPTER 6

WHERE WE ARE NOW

In Part 1, I wanted to lay it all out there. My hope was to give you an idea of what happened for me, what it meant about my life, and how my perception of my circumstances affected me for over twenty years.

But the biggest reason I feel called to share my story is to connect us on a deeper level. As I've opened up more and more about my past over the years, I've come to realize the inherent strength of being vulnerable and letting people into my world.

When people are open and willing to share a piece of themselves, their connection to one another will undoubtedly grow stronger. That powerful connection isn't born in the exchanged sympathy; feeling sorry for each other doesn't necessarily foster a better relationship. Rather, our associations are strengthened by how much we hear and see ourselves in the narratives of other people's lives.

Hopefully, as you read through how the events of my childhood affected my relationships, my finances, my career, and my spirituality over the years, the pages in your hand became a mirror. You looked down and saw words on a page, but, in reality, the reflection you took in was yourself. Your dad may not have died, but you've dealt with your own version of pain. You've told yourself stories about what circumstances meant to you, what they meant about you, and you've carried those stories for a while without knowing how to put them down. And since you've walked a path that parallels mine in some way, our bond now has a depth that wasn't present on page one.

But we're not here to swap more sob stories and double down on how unfair life is. Filling a book with negative energy wouldn't serve the purpose I promised. From here on out, let's talk about how to *change our stories*. Let's discuss what it looks like to rise from the ashes and take back the life we thought no longer belonged to us.

In Part 2 of this book, I'm going to share the who, the what, and the how of getting past the pain that's been holding you back.

There are a few people in my life who have made it possible for me to step out of a dark past and into a bigger, brighter future. I'll be introducing you to these people and showing you how to find people who will challenge and support you as you grow into the fullest version of yourself.

Apart from the people who lit this path for me, there were several environments I sought out that shifted my perspective on what life is all about. If I hadn't immersed myself in those spaces of safety and growth, I'm not sure I'd be here writing this book. In this section, we'll spend some time finding places you can and should seek out to help you rise to the next level in your life.

Finally, this section of the book will discuss how these people and these places allowed me to start thinking new thoughts. It may sound like a small and simple shift, but your thoughts really do create your reality. I spent many years waiting for my outer world to change but didn't take the time to change what I was thinking and believing in my inner world.

When this portion of the book is complete, you'll be equipped with more empowering ways to think, speak, and believe so you can shift out of pain and into living a life of purpose.

Are you ready? Good. Let's do this!

CHAPTER 7

HOW PEOPLE HELPED MY PROGRESS

You take yourself with you everywhere you go.

I didn't get that for a very, very long time. In an attempt to escape the pain I was living in, I switched jobs, travelled, and moved around quite a bit in early adulthood. I thought if I could change my scenery, somehow the story about my life would change. But what I didn't realize was that as I scrambled the setting of my life, I carried a large suitcase around with the word PAIN emblazoned across the front. Whether I was moving across town or shipping off for a tropical vacation, that big ol' suitcase always came along for the ride.

My pain—well, my story about my pain—popped up over and over again, often at the most inopportune times. I'd get a new job and somehow sabotage my way into getting fired. I'd get a new place to live, excited about the fresh start away from the trauma and drama, and somehow get sucked back into what I was trying to escape. I'd meet a new girl and begin to build what I thought was a stable relationship only to watch it crumble.

I thought I could outrun my pain, but it kept pace like

a champ. You'd think I would notice the patterns and stop trying to fix my world from the outside in. No matter what I changed or switched out externally, though, my internal turmoil steered each new venture into a ditch. I put off fixing my heart and soul, thinking if I could just figure out how to maximize my material world, I could finally find some peace and happiness within. You know that game, right?

I'll be happy *when* someone loves me.
I'll be joyful *when* I have a ton of money in the bank.
I'll be content *when* I find the perfect job.

I was forever trying to pull in people, places, and things from outside of myself to make me feel whole, not realizing that the path to wholeness actually moved in the opposite direction.

Happiness wasn't going to be the result of meeting the right person, it would be the reason why the right person would want to hang out with me in the first place. I needed to find my way to happiness *first*.

The money in the bank wouldn't produce joy in my life (not in a deep and fulfilling way, anyway). I needed to be joyful *first*, then go out and do work that lit me up. The cash flow would follow.

There was no perfect job for a guy in extreme pain, so waiting for one to give me the contentment I desired was a fool's errand. I needed to commit to being content with myself; then I'd find a job I would enjoy.

I was going the wrong way down a one-way street trying to find the life I desired, and I had no idea. I kept thinking the perfect job, the perfect vacation, or a stack of cash would enable me to put down that gigantic suitcase marked PAIN at some point. But I just kept lugging that damn case with me everywhere I went.

And after the all the trouble it had caused me, something good finally came from it. I met the girl of my dreams.

It was 2007, and I was ready for something more. I knew it was time to stop living my life as a victim and to become the victor of the years I had left. I was ready to let my pain dissolve and to allow more beauty into my life. I was eager for a life that wasn't defined by everything I had endured—to create something on my own terms. I had no idea what a better life looked like, but I knew I was ready for it. I didn't have the slightest clue how I would shake a couple of decades' worth of pain and trauma, but I was willing to do everything I could to figure it out.

Since I was ignorant of how to move from my pain to a life of purpose, I decided to head to Cabo with the boys to clear my head. I hoped the sun and the sand might give me the physical and mental space to think about what I needed to do to change my life for the better. I packed my bags, including my trusty PAIN luggage, and headed out.

I thought I was going to paradise to clear my head and to think through what to do next. As it turned out, my head had nothing to do with it. In Cabo, I discovered that my heart was the key to the life I wanted.

In Cabo, I met the love of my life, Lori.

I couldn't put my finger on what it was about her, but as soon as we met, I knew there was something different, something I needed in my life. She gave me a sense of calm I had never experienced. To my recollection, I had almost never enjoyed a conscious moment of relaxation due to all my stress. I was always anxious and absolutely certain life would throw me back into a tornado of pain at a moment's notice. With Lori, though, I felt at ease.

We connected almost instantly, and I ended up spending most of my trip trying to get closer to this woman who had my full attention. As our vacation wound down and we went our separate ways, we exchanged numbers and said we'd keep in touch. Little did I know that within three months of landing back in Texas, I would be moving to California to start my life with this incredible woman.

I went to Cabo looking for a way to bring my life out of the darkness and into the light, and I got exactly what—or more accurately, who—I needed. But if I hadn't been ready for her, it wouldn't have mattered. If I hadn't met Lori, I don't know if I'd be writing this book. But if I hadn't prepared my heart to open for her, meeting her wouldn't have been enough.

Sure, she was—and still is—beautiful. She made me laugh; she made me forget about all the pain and suffering I went to Cabo to abandon. But a stat sheet of all her endearing qualities wouldn't do justice to what she means to me and the shift that occurred in my life after meeting her.

Lori saw through my stories and believed in a version of me I had forsaken—or never known. Amazing! The stories that I deeply believed to be factual, she recognized were fictional.

I believed I didn't deserve love. She knew I did.

I thought I was meant to struggle. She showed me I didn't have to.

I assumed I was trapped forever on a roller coaster of pain, grief, and anger for the rest of my life. She allowed me to hop off the ride.

She was the catalyst to everything I've created in my life since then. Now, she didn't do all the work for me, of course. Ultimately, I had to decide to honor her support and to realize the potential she saw in me. But having a loving, graceful presence like her by my side made it a hell of a lot easier. There was always a small fire inside me that desired to make the most of what life I had left, but getting to know Lori poured gasoline all over it, and the flame hasn't faded since.

If you want to go fast, go alone.
If you want to go far, go together.

~ African Proverb

I spent many years keeping people at arm's length and thought I could get by all on my own. I didn't want to burden anyone with my baggage, and I sure as hell didn't need more sympathy from anyone. As it turns out, letting people in was the missing piece in the puzzle of my life that I simply had to embrace to understand. When I met Lori, I knew I would make it work no matter what. She drew me in like no one ever had, but there was an admission price to the happiness she represented: I had to open up and let her into my world. Despite it scaring me half to death, her grace provided a safe space, so I put it all on the table.

I waited for it to bite me in the ass. I assumed at some point she'd look at me and say, "I'm sorry, Jay, you're beyond repair," and take off with some guy that had his shit together. But she never did. Instead of rejecting me and deepening my wounds, she helped me heal.

She was the one who showed me how powerful it is to have supportive people in your life. If you follow me on social media or if you read my first book, *The Overweight Mind*, you know that one of my pillars of living a successful life is surrounding yourself with what I call a Circle of Success. Having people to lean on when you're feeling weak and to cheer you on when you're feeling strong is essential not only to healing your pain but also to rising above it and thriving in your life.

You can fight this idea all you want, but if you attempt to navigate your pain by yourself, you will likely never find the light at the end of the tunnel.

You need people to tell you that your stories about yourself aren't true.

You need people to lift you up when you don't have the strength or courage to stand.

You need people to inspire you to see past the pain and suffering you've grown accustomed to.

Lori offered that to me, and once I allowed myself to accept her support, my life took off. My support system is bigger than just her these days, with coaches, mentors, friends, and family rounding out my Circle of Success. They keep me in check. They keep me inspired. They continue to show me that I am worthy of everything I am striving toward. I would still be stuck in the struggle if I hadn't embraced my great community.

Again, human beings are an interpersonal species, with tribes and communities being a staple of civilization for as long as we've existed on this planet. We need each other. Rejecting that premise and trying to solve all of your problems without support is just fighting human nature.

If you're in pain right now, seek out your own Circle of Success. Find a friend or family member you can confide in and let it all out. Seek out support groups that will allow you to talk about your stories; get those sad tales out of your body. Look for other people who have gone through similar circumstances and ask them what solutions they uncovered.

Will it be one of the scariest things you've ever done? You can bet your sweet ass it will. Will it be the most healing thing you've ever done for yourself in the long run? When you find the right people, it will be more healing than you could ever imagine.

There is no one on this planet who deserves to suffer alone and in silence. Speak your truth to someone you feel comfortable with. Understand, it will be terrifying, but it will eventually free you from the prison your stories have created over the years.

It's time to break free, my friend. Just know you can't do it alone.

CHAPTER 8

HOW CHANGING MY ENVIRONMENT HELPED MY PROGRESS

"I can't wait to get there!"
"This is so dumb."
"This is going to change everything."
"I swear to God, if they tell me to believe in myself, I'm gonna puke."
"It's time. I'm ready. This is the first day of the rest of my life."
"I can't believe I'm actually going to this thing. Lori's lucky she's cute."

That was my inner dialogue as Lori and I drove up to my first ever personal development conference. The old me would have pointed and laughed at anyone gullible enough to throw their money at a self-help conference, but since I trusted Lori's judgment and she wanted to go, I happily tagged along.

Despite my initial reservations about sitting in a huge ballroom with five hundred other people looking for answers to whatever big questions they were asking, part of me was excited to see what would come of our time at the seminar—the part that was ready to move past all of my pain and generate some positive momentum toward a life I could truly enjoy.

But the lingering residue of the old me—the piece of me whose fuel source was ego and fear—was resistant. That part of me thought all this "self-helpy" stuff was a crock. But that was really just my fear. I was scared, terrified I might enjoy the stuff I'd always talked smack about. Scared it might bring up some of my past that I was desperately trying to flee. But mostly, I was scared that the overall message of the event would be true, and I would no longer have the sacred excuses I had held on to for a long time.

What was that message, you ask? Well, it was summed up in one sentence:

You can be, do, and have everything you desire.

The guy who spoke those words from the main stage said it with such confidence that even I had a hard time trying to prove him wrong. Trust me, my ego definitely wanted to. I wanted to scream, "What about desiring that my dad comes back to life?" But every other part of me wanted to believe what he said was true. I wanted to trust in the idea that I could be, do, and have anything I wanted. Because if that one sentence ended up being true, I could pivot my life of pain into a life of love, prosperity, and abundance.

Despite my hope I could have whatever I wanted, believing that notion any time soon was a little far-fetched. Until that point, I had spent a couple of decades experiencing exactly what I didn't want, so I couldn't just snap my fingers and suddenly be, do, and have everything I wanted.

As I reflect on those words, I know having Lori next to me as I heard them played a big role in my believing in them. She was proof I could have *something* I wanted, so maybe... just maybe...I could find success in other parts of my life.

Over the next few days at the conference, I slid back and forth between my story of pain and my story of potential. One moment, I was inspired; the next I was back to my old self. But I recognized something: even though I could not make my mental and emotional load disappear with a snap of my fingers, I knew my burden was lessening. Every time resistance grew and I felt myself slipping back into a state of fear and frustration, I would repeat the words that had struck me like lightning on the first day of the conference:

You can be, do, and have everything you desire.

With each repetition of the phrase, I chipped away at the weighty narrative I had been living, the one telling me to stay trapped in a life full of misery and sadness.

If I started to feel down about the years I wasted being

angry about my circumstances, I would say to myself, *You can be, do, and have everything you desire.*

When fear told me I did not deserve to turn my life around, when self-doubt whispered that I was doomed to repeat my cycle of pain and suffering, I would stop whatever I was doing and say, Y*ou can be, do, and have everything you desire.*

If my old patterns and stories started to bubble up, I would cut them off and come back to the message: *You can be, do, and have everything that you desire.*

Had I been back home on the couch trying to repeat that phrase to myself, I doubt it would have stuck. Being in the energy of the seminar—surrounded by other people who were open to the reality of being, doing, and having anything they wanted—allowed me to lean into the words. The more I repeated them, the greater shot they had at being true.

I needed that level of hope. I needed to believe there was an alternative to the despair and depression I had been experiencing for decades. The seminar created an environment of protection for my desire to do more with my life; it put me in close proximity to other people who were on the same path. If someone had told me I could be, do, and have anything I desired while I was still living in Texas—an environment constantly pounding me with the opposite perspective—there is zero chance I would have held onto the hope of those words.

But being in the conference center for three straight days

allowed my mind to sit with the message and feel its truth. Today, the phrase is a core belief of mine. I live and breathe it every day. It has become as true to me as the fact that my name is Jay and I'm a dude. I have seen the validity of being, doing, and having everything I desire because after years and years of putting it to the test, I keep stepping into more and more of what I want. It's a mantra I now teach to my clients, a reality I remind them of every day. I know if they latch onto it and truly believe it, the words will transform their world. The environment and energy of the conference gave me the space and support I needed to believe in the message, and now I get to create a similar space for my clients every single day.

Aside from being in a new energy of possibility and abundance, those three days at my first personal development conference gave me a ton of perspective. I entered the event believing my story was too big and scary to overcome, but I discovered my past and my pain had some competition.

There was a moment when we all sat in a room with two microphones set up in the middle of it. People were encouraged to step up to the microphone and share their stories, knowing there was a room full of people ready to support them in their vulnerability.

With each person who stepped up, I'd think to myself, "There's no way their story is as devastating as mine." And almost every single time, I was wrong. There's a quote that used to drive me nuts. It made me cringe because of how wrong I believed it was:

If we all threw our problems into a pile, and saw everyone else's, we'd take ours back.[4]

~ Regina Brett

I always thought it was a cute little quip that applied to everyone else who hadn't been to hell and back. But here I was in this room full of strangers sharing their stories, and all I could think of was how my life hadn't been so bad. If everyone in that room tossed their stories into a pile of sadness, death, and destruction, there's a decent chance I would've looked for mine if I had to pick through the rubble.

The gift of perspective took me off my high horse of pain. It allowed me to see that all living, breathing people have their own pain—and they are working through it. I was so convinced my pain was special, that my story excused me from making the most of my life. I could always just play the "my dad died when I was five" card. But that conference room showed me my story wasn't as isolated and separate from the norm as I thought.

---

4 Regina Brett, "Regina Brett's 45 Life Lessons and 5 to Grow On," *Cleveland Plain Dealer* (May 28, 2006), https://www.cleveland.com/brett/blog/2006/05/regina_bretts_45_life_lessons.html

I learned a valuable lesson: pain is subjective. It hurt like hell for me, but everyone else who shared their story had clearly gone through their own version of mental, emotional, and sometimes physical torture. I realized I wasn't alone in my struggle to understand my path through pain, because everyone had their own weighty version.

Here's what I learned at the conference: Pain is not about the objective events or circumstances at all. It's about what that event or circumstance means to the landscape of our individual lives. My dad meant a lot to me as a five-year-old boy, so obviously his death and subsequent absence in my life crushed me. His loss was tragic, but the meaning I created made his death almost unlivable. While total strangers talked, I realized almost all of them had marinated in their own pain as I had soaked in mine. My judgment of everyone else's trauma faded with each new story I heard. I began to feel something I had never encountered in my life: compassion.

My first personal development conference changed my life. It put me in a supportive environment; it shored up every vulnerable spot and made me ready for change. I was challenged to think bigger than I ever had before. It's hard to imagine that anything could stick from a three-day experience. How could a long weekend really stay with me for well over a decade?

Well, it did, and it represents a turning point; it brought on complete transformation.

What made the conference so meaningful was an exercise at the beginning that was meant to allow us to carry the conference's energy everywhere we went. In fact, I still carry it in my wallet.

Let me explain.

On the first day of the seminar, we were given a dollar bill and told to hold onto it. No one told us anything more, so I just tucked it away in my wallet and forgot about it. I had no idea how much something so simple and ordinary would impact my life. The piece of paper is only worth one dollar in the marketplace, but its value to me cannot be estimated.

Over the course of the three-day stint, I began to trust the message and energy of what I was experiencing. I was slowly but surely opening myself up to a world where change was possible, but I had my doubts about whether everything would stick. I was a little skeptical about my ability to continue the hype once I stepped back into the real world. My conscious mind was pumped up by the potential of what could happen for me moving forward, but my subconscious mind kept trying to rerun my stories of fear and uncertainty. I needed a sign. I needed something to declare a winner in the fight between my excitement for the new life I was ready to create and my doubts of it ever really happening.

Then, they turned the lights off.

Everyone in the conference was suddenly sitting in the dark. A voice echoed in the gloom. "Find the dollar bill you were given." I fumbled in my wallet and wondered, "What the hell?" I pulled it out and immediately understood what was happening. Like headlights cutting through a dark night, there were two words printed on my dollar bill with glow-in-the-dark ink:

Just Believe.

I'd needed a sign, and they had presented one on my first day. The seemingly insignificant gift of a dollar provided a monumental signal that allowed me to trust in everything I wanted to be, do, and have.

I needed to believe that what I was experiencing was my new normal. I needed to believe I could shed my pain and find the purpose within it. I needed to believe that Lori was not too good to be true. I needed a nudge from the Universe telling me the life I was dreaming about at the conference was not make believe—that it could happen.

CHAPTER 9

HOW CHANGING MY THOUGHTS HELPED MY PROGRESS

I vividly remember the first time I saw the movie The Secret.[5]

I can hear you now: "Oh boy, here we go. Jay's going to tell us all about how thoughts make things..."

Now, stay with me here. Put your opinions of the Law of Attraction aside for a moment and just hear me out. Like you, I was skeptical when I heard about the movie. The idea that I could create the life I desired through thought alone just seemed like a crock of shit to ole Jay. Given what I had gone through, I had a hard time wrapping my mind around something so totally opposite of my experience and belief. I could "think" all I wanted—nothing was going to bring my father back or restore my family. It would be a tall task for someone or something to convince me otherwise.

But I found *The Secret* when I was open to trying new things, when I was ready to create change in my life—even something that sounded a little nutty. After meeting Lori and attending the personal development conference with her, I

---

5 Rhonda Byrne, dir, *The Secret*, Prime Time Productions, 2006.

was more ready than ever to explore life in a different way. If someone had told me about *The Secret* a year earlier, there's no chance I would have watched it. Here I was, though, posted up with my popcorn and a side of doubt, ready to see what this thing was all about.

And I absolutely loved it.

I loved it in the same way you love a Disney movie, though. The story moved me, inspired me, and made me wish it were true. But deep down, a part of me thought it was all just a fairy tale; it could never work for me.

In keeping with the theme of this season of my life, though, I remained open to it even if I had trouble getting on board right away. I touched my wallet several times while listening to story after story during the movie, reminding myself: *Just Believe.* Maybe, just maybe, this stuff wasn't as fictional as I perceived it to be.

One idea really grabbed me: the concept of vision boards. I remember John Assaraf looking into the camera and telling the audience about all the things he had compiled on his. He had cars, travel adventures, and his dream house on his display. He looked at it daily. He would envision himself driving those cars, taking those trips, and living in that house. Time passed and he found increasing success in his career and life; eventually, he moved into a large home in the Arizona desert. As he unpacked his boxes at the new place, he pulled out his vision board and stared at it. When he was reminded of everything he had cut out and taped to the poster board, the memories brought him to tears. He had just moved into the house he had placed on his vision board five years prior! Not a similar house. Not another mansion in the same neighborhood. *The same house!*

Stories like Assaraf's really made me dig into what *The Secret* was offering. The concept of visualizing goals and transferring them from thought to reality fascinated me. I'd never heard anything like it. It was absolutely foreign to me, but I loved it. I made my very own vision board. I went big and bold, placing things on the board that my conscious mind thought I had no business trying to acquire. But I was riding high from the energy I got from watching *The Secret*, and as my eyes closed every night moving forward, I envisioned what my life would be like when all my goals were achieved.

The movie really cracked my mind open. I had lived my life thinking I was trapped in my circumstances, but *The Secret*'s perspective flipped every notion I had on its head. I realized a great truth: events had not built prison walls around me—the walls came from me and my thoughts.

I thought I was doomed to live in despair, so despair found its way to me over and over again.

I thought loving someone meant you'd eventually lose them, so my life produced the evidence to validate the proposition.

I thought I wasn't going to be alive for long, that planning for the future wasn't a priority, so anytime I built a foundation for what could be my future, I watched it crumble before my eyes.

I thought I had no control over my life's path, so I generated all the chaos I kept experiencing.

I had my guard up when the movie began, but by the time the credits rolled, I was ready to investigate the possibilities. I grabbed any book I could find that touched on what I'd seen—anything about mindset, personal development, and the idea that your thoughts can create the world around you had my full attention.

Looking back on my time of blissful curiosity, one book stands above the rest. It's a book that I still learn from to this day: *Manifesting Your Destiny: The Nine Spiritual Principles for Getting Everything You Want by Dr. Wayne Dyer*[6]. Each page held a sentence, a quotation, or an idea challenging how I saw the world. It woke me up to what I had been missing as I tried to rise from the ashes of my past. Some of the words in particular spoke to my heart and soul in a way I'd never experienced. They inspired me and seized hold of the part that was ready to see and to experience things differently. As I share these with you over the next few pages, I hope

6 Wayne Dyer, *Manifesting Your Destiny: The Nine Spiritual Principles for Getting Everything You Want*, (New York: HarperCollins, 1997).

they meet you in a moment you need them most, like they did for me.

Let's look at a few.

► *Everything is either an opportunity to grow or an obstacle to keep you from growing. You get to choose.*

This quote offered a new lens through which to see my life. I won't lie, I was resistant when I first read those words. I knew I didn't have a choice in the matter of my dad's death or any other subsequent tragedy. However, I never considered the possibility that I had a choice to see those events as opportunities to grow. I just assumed the only option available was to allow them to stand as enormous obstacles in my life. Since I thought they were roadblocks, I experienced roadblocks. As it turns out, I had other options.

Once I allowed myself to entertain the idea that everything I'd gone through offered me an opportunity to grow, I was back in the driver's seat of my life. I couldn't go back and change the past, but I started to see it differently. Instead of looking for more reasons to wallow in my sorrow, I started to see those dark moments as places I'd survived despite the hell I endured. Nothing would bring my dad back to life, but I saw his death as an opportunity to become resilient, strong, and compassionate.

▶ *You cannot always control what goes on outside. But you can always control what goes on inside.*

The first part of this quote was easy enough to understand. Throughout the course of my life, I was shown time and time again how little control I had over what happened around me. The second half, however, caused some conflict in my heart and mind. It was hard for me to grasp that I had any sort of control over how I felt about my circumstances.

I believed my emotional state and inner being were simply reactions to whatever I was experiencing externally. I never thought I had a choice in the matter. If I felt sad, I imagined my emotions reflected a sad event. If I felt happy, the joy was connected to some event or person making me feel that way. But after sitting with this new idea for a while, I realized the events of my life *influenced* how I felt inside, but they never had the final say in how I felt.

I did.

I had the right and the opportunity to respond to my environment differently; I just never realized I had the option. Today I understand that not many circumstances stand in the way of me feeling how I want to feel and living how I want to live.

▶ *You are not stuck where you are unless you decide to be.*

If you're anything like me, this one's going to sting a bit once you really wrap your head around it. I could write an entire book about moments in my life when I felt stuck. My life was shattered when I was a little kid, and I spent a long time being frustrated about the mess my dad left for me. It kept me distant from other people. It kept me scared to live life fully. It kept me angry. I wanted to be dealt a better hand.

But my dad's death didn't keep me stuck. I did. I chose to leave the pieces of my life scattered on the floor. I chose to lament my circumstances instead of trying to change them. I chose to close myself off from other people and to bottle up my pain. My dad didn't do that. My mom didn't do that. No one decided how things would play out—except me.

You are not stuck. That's a hard pill to swallow, but it was a prescription I desperately needed. As my relationship with Lori developed and blossomed, I was at a crossroads. It was time to find the next level. Once things began to fall into place for me, I never wanted to feel stuck again. I had a new goal—being "un-stuck." The future belonged to me—not to my past, not to my pain. To me!

► *Change the way you look at things and the things you look at change.*

When I received the news of my father's sudden death, I was custom-fit with a new set of blinders. For decades, I focused only on tragedy and trauma. I was immersed in a world where grief was the *status quo*, and everyone was just waiting around for the next terrible event to come to pass. From the moment I woke up until the moment I closed my tear-filled eyes at night, all I saw was pain.

It took a while for pain to loosen its grip on me, allowing me to see there was more to life than death and destruction. Once those blinders came off, I saw pain in context, as part of a bigger picture.

I understood I wasn't alone in my pain. There were plenty of other people with their own stuff to work through. I wasn't the only one cursed by a series of unfortunate events.

I also saw that my pain had a purpose. When my blinders were on, all I saw were people dying. When I opened up my view of the world, all I saw were more reasons to live. The pain and suffering I'd endured provided me contrast. It gave me an idea of exactly what I didn't want to experience as I grew older. Without that contrast, I wouldn't be so fulfilled by the life of abundance and joy I've created.

Once I started to look at my pain differently, I felt differently about it. It didn't weigh me down anymore. In fact, it provided the fuel I needed to shift my life to a level I had previously thought impossible. But that never would have happened if I had kept those blinders on. You will always get more of what you focus on. Once I chose to focus on a life that didn't center around the pain I'd been experiencing,

I found a way to move past it with purpose.

► *The more you see yourself as what you'd like to become, and act as if what you want is already there, the more you'll activate those dormant forces that will collaborate to transform your dream into your reality.*

The most important part of this quote to me are the words "act as if." I left that personal development conference with the mantra "You can be, do, and have anything you desire" tattooed on my soul. I wanted to believe it. I wanted it to be true. As I read this thought from Dr. Dyer, I realized it wasn't a matter of wishing it were true...I had to "act as if" it already was.

I had to step into the shoes of the guy I wanted to become and start living life from his perspective, rather than waiting for things to fall into place for me. To be the person I wanted to become, I had to jump into a better state of being and operate there. To do the things I wanted to accomplish in my life, I needed to start working on them. I couldn't wait until I was ready to do them; I had to do what I could with what I had and figure it out along the way. To have the things I desired, I had to think deeply about why those things mattered to me, how they could improve my life, and what was necessary to acquire them.

I had to shift my perspective from hoping and dreaming to living in my "future place." Once I began to visualize what my life would be like, once I began to spend time there, my world began to mold itself to fit what I was envisioning.

► *When you're at peace with yourself and love yourself, it is virtually impossible to do things to yourself that are destructive.*

This one hit me really hard. I felt its truth as I read the words on the page, but my mind didn't want to give in just yet. I was resistant to the quotation's sentiment because it was in complete conflict with how I had been living my life. Inner peace was a foreign concept to me for the vast majority of my life. My outer world was chaotic, and I allowed my inner world to reflect the same chaos. Without a sense of inner peace, and with a severe lack of self-love, my destructive behaviors kept popping up. More often than not, I'd sabotage any form of success and find my way back to my misery.

As Lori got to know me, she said something that sticks in my head and heart to this day: "I have never met anyone who is as hard on themselves as you are." All the actions I took were reflective of the pain and chaos I had inside. I didn't work out to get healthy. I hit the gym because I loathed the chubby kid I believed myself to be. I didn't end relationships because I didn't like the person I was with. I ended them because I didn't like the person that I was, and I felt the other person could do better.

I was my own worst critic. After reading this quotation, though, I realized I needed to become my biggest cheerleader. I desperately wanted to feel loved and accepted by others. I realize now that others were only going to care about me *after* I learned how to care about myself. I spent years slamming my life into a metaphorical wall because I thought if I just kept going hard enough, I'd bust through to the other side. Once I really committed to loving and accepting myself, finding a level of inner peace I never dreamt possible, the wall crumbled.

▶ *Each experience in your life was absolutely necessary to move you to the next place, and up to this very moment.*

By now you're probably sensing a trend with these quotations. When you read them objectively, the powerful words can shift and shape your world for the better. When I read them subjectively—from the point of view that included all the shit I had gone through—each of them triggered me in some way. This particular one probably gave me the most trouble. Now remember, I was open and ready to accept new ways of thought back when I read this book by Dr. Wayne Dyer, but this felt like a little too much. If I accepted these words as truth, I wouldn't just be accepting my dad's death and its role in my life. I would have to believe they were absolutely necessary. Needless to say, there was some resistance on my end.

But without my dad's death, I know I wouldn't be where I am today. I just can't picture how I would be able to show up as I am without going through what I've experienced. All the death, despair, and depression created decades' worth of contrast; they showed me exactly what I didn't want in my life. I wanted love, safety, security, and abundance, and those dark years after Dad died showed me what the opposite of those feelings were. I had the blueprint for a life I didn't want; from that place, I was able to seek its opposite. You can't truly enjoy the sunshine until you've been caught in a thunderstorm or two. Sure, it took a long time, but if I hadn't stood in that storm and experienced the grief that came with it, I wouldn't have such gratitude for the life I've created now.

► *The state of your life is nothing more than a reflection of the state of your mind.*

I think it's natural for human beings to get caught up in the world outside of ourselves. When we are lonely, we hop on Match.com or Tinder to see if we can find someone to fill the void. If we are broke, we try our hardest to make more money.

If we find ourselves 100 pounds overweight, we immediately look to eat less and workout more. We're constantly trying to manipulate our circumstances to move our lives to the next level. But as I wrote about in *The Overweight Mind* and as Dyer communicates in this quote, nothing will shift permanently in your physical world until you change something in your mental, emotional, and spiritual worlds.

Admittedly, back when I was struggling, I kept waiting for my life to change without realizing I had to change first. It wasn't until I started to shift my mindset and to open myself up to new ways of thought and belief that my world finally shifted into high gear. Prior to my internal transformation, no change ever stuck. Once I upgraded my state of mind, the world around me upgraded as well.

▶ *If we focus on what's ugly, we attract more ugliness into our thoughts, and then into our emotions, and ultimately into our lives.*

This last thought continues a theme that weaves through most of the others listed here: you have more control over your life than you think you do. Line after line from Dr. Dyer's book smacked me in the face with that truth. Just a few months before reading Dyer's book, I deeply believed I had little to no control over how my life played out. I thought everything I had experienced was just plain bad luck. As it turns out, I had more to do with my situation than I thought.

I spent years focusing on the ugly parts of my life, and true to Dyer's point, more ugly stuff came my way. The more I gave my attention to the wreckage of my life, the more evidence I would find that things would never get better.

My focus, my mindset, and my inner world were all things I could control. I just never realized they could affect the world I see around me. I thought everything inside—my emotions, my thoughts, my beliefs, my attitude—were completely separate from the world I observed through my eyeballs. But after exposing myself to *Manifesting Your Destiny: The Nine Spiritual Principles for Getting Everything You Want*, I quickly realized they were very much intertwined.

Understanding I had a lot to do with the results I was experiencing was simultaneously exciting and embarrassing. On one hand, I was thrilled I could shift the path of the rest of my life by optimizing my thoughts, beliefs, and emotions. On the other hand, I couldn't help but think I had wasted a couple of decades wallowing in sorrow when I could have shifted out of it.

But as much as I wanted to beat myself up for not taking advantage of the power inside, I knew it wouldn't do any good. That's the thing about the past and the pain—you can never change what happened, but you can change what you do with it. I couldn't go back and change my previous path any more than I could bring my dad back to life. Truth be told, if I could change my path or my dad's death, I might have steered myself away from my current life. My pain and my past weren't pretty, but they led me to a place in my life where I was ready for new people, new environments, and new thoughts.

I met Lori when I was supposed to. I went to that conference when I was supposed to. I came across *The Secret* and the work of Dr. Wayne Dyer when I was supposed to.

Maybe you're coming across this book when you're supposed to. Maybe the pain you've walked through has made you more ready and willing for a new way of life than ever before. As much as you may want to shrink back into your story of pain and suffering, know that the changes you will experience if you stay the course of this book are meant for you. Nothing has found you by mistake.

As the dollar bill still residing in my wallet will tell you…

…Just Believe.

CHAPTER 10

BEWARE THE PERSONAL DEVELOPMENT VORTEX

I met new people, opened my mind to new ideas, and put myself in environments that fostered and nurtured my willingness to progress through my pain. I'd worn my pain like a badge of honor for a couple of decades. When I was finally ready to move past it, though, those new thoughts, inspiring people, and supportive environments were the reason I was able to get strong footing on my new path.

But before you head to Amazon to find a life-changing book or search for the next local event that might take your life to the next level, I need to warn you. There is no participation trophy in personal development. You aren't gifted amazing results simply by attending a seminar or listening to a podcast.

I can guarantee there are people who were present at the same conference I attended back in the day who are still stuck. I promise you there are other people who read Dr. Wayne Dyer's book *Manifesting Your Destiny: The Nine Spiritual Principles for Getting Everything You Want* who haven't manifested a damn thing. I will bet you $1 million cash there are people who saw *The Secret* and still haven't attracted what they desire into their lives.

It's not about how much personal development you expose yourself to, it's about how much personal development you use. There is an infinite amount of information out there on how to live a better life. But building up a stat sheet of all the books you've read, all the podcasts you've listened to, and all the conferences you've attended is essentially useless...unless you've implemented the things you've learned from them.

This is what I need to warn you about. The endless drive for more information—without taking the time to integrate any of it—is what I call the "Personal Development Vortex." It sucks you in, and if you're not careful, you'll never come out with the results you thought you were working toward.

The worst part about it is that it makes you feel like you're doing something right. You're reading all the books your favorite guru recommended. You're listening to every powerful podcast episode you can get your hands on...twice. You're paying top dollar for VIP tickets to the biggest and best conferences centered on personal growth and transformation. With all the energy you're pouring into the field of personal development, you're bound to experience some amazing changes, right?

Well, no. There is no guarantee in the information alone. The only way to make something of it is to put it to work.

I didn't get where I am in life simply because I read a powerful book or went to an amazing conference. I created the shifts in my life because I implemented and embodied the messages I learned. I still carry that dollar bill that says *Just Believe t*o remind me of my first conference and what I learned there. There are quotations from the Dr. Wayne Dyer book I continually lean on when I'm guiding my clients through their own seasons of transformation. Everything I've mentioned in this section of the book—meeting new people, reading new books, being in new environments—holds power. That power only became mine to use, though, once I embodied, believed in, and integrated every single thing I'd learned.

How did I do it? How did I avoid the Personal Development Vortex and sidestep spending year after year running in circles trying to find the next best thing to improve my life? What's my secret?

Frankly, there isn't one. There is no secret. There is no best way to live your life and no one way of moving through your pain on the way to purpose.

There are plenty of gurus, authors, and influencers who will send you on a wild goose chase trying to find that one magic trick guaranteed to solve all of your problems. They benefit from you looking for the shiniest, newest way to live your best life. Why? Because it gives them a new book to write.

I'm not interested in leading you blindly into an infinite search for the next best thing. I want you to get what you came for: a solution to your problems. In this case, a way to find purpose in the pain of your past or your present.

That solution will never be found in one singular act. If it were, I would end the book right here and tell you what you should do next. Instead, I'll be real with you: The path to your purpose is a process. It's one you're going to have to fall in love with because the process never ends.

Meeting Lori changed my life and the way I saw love and relationships, but I'm still trying to get better as her partner. Finding books filled with powerful ideas about abundance and prosperity changed the way I see wealth and business, but I'm still learning how to optimize how I make and spend money. Getting around supportive people was essential, but I'm always looking to build upon my Circle of Success.

At some point I had an itch to get better in life, and I've been scratching that itch ever since. Every day I look to improve my relationship, my health, and my business, even though I'm light-years ahead of where I used to be.

That's just it: the only way to avoid the Personal Development Vortex is to act continuously and to integrate everything you're consuming. I read books all the time, then I apply what my eyeballs take in. I go to conferences every year, but I never walk away from them without a plan to put what I learned into action. I have coaches and mentors, but I don't invest in them just to share my receipt on Instagram. I put everything to use, and because of that, my life has grown exponentially since I started down this path so long ago.

So, before we hit the ground running in Part 3 of this book and dig into some tactical things you can use to shift from a place of pain to one of purpose, I'm going to do everything I can to make sure you don't trip and fall into the Personal Development Vortex. The last thing I want you to do is to read the rest of this book for sport, tell someone how powerful it was, and then plug into your next podcast.

I want you to put this stuff to use!

Use the space provided below to do an audit of your personal development activities over the last six to twelve months. If this is your first foray into the genre, keep this exercise in mind as you move forward.

The practice is simple. I still use this format today to get clear on why I'm engaging with any form of content or any environment. It frames my mind around the result I am seeking from each experience, allowing me to engage below the surface-level nonsense of most personal development junkies.

Bring honesty to the exercise. If you find that you're reading books or listening to podcasts just to bulk up your stat sheet, allow this to be a place where you can pivot to a more valuable experience.

PERSONAL DEVELOPMENT AUDIT

1. Seminars: List the last three seminars you attended along with your purpose for attending and the actions you took after attending that moved you forward in life.

Seminar: ______________________________

Purpose: ______________________________

Actions: ______________________________

Seminar: ______________________________

Purpose: ______________________________

Actions: ______________________________

Seminar: ______________________________

Purpose: ______________________________

Actions: ______________________________

2. Books: List the last three personal development, self-help, or motivational books you read along with the purpose for reading and the actions you took after finishing the book that moved you forward in life.

Book: ______________________________

Purpose: ______________________________

Actions: ______________________________

Book: ______________________________

Purpose: ______________________________

Actions: ______________________________

Book: ______________________________

Purpose: ______________________________

Actions: ______________________________

3. Podcasts: List the last three personal development, self-help, or motivational podcasts you listened to along with the purpose for listening and the actions you took after finishing that moved you forward in life.

Podcast: ______________________________

Purpose: ______________________________

Actions: ______________________________

Podcast: ______________________________

Purpose: ______________________________

Actions: ______________________________

Podcast: ______________________________

Purpose: ______________________________

Actions: ______________________________

4. Coach/Mentor: List your last three coaches/mentors along with your purpose for working with them and the critical actions you've taken since receiving their advice.

Coach/Mentor: ______________________________

Purpose: ______________________________

Actions: ______________________________

Coach/Mentor: ______________________________

Purpose: ______________________________

Actions: ______________________________

Coach/Mentor: ______________________________

Purpose: ______________________________

Actions: ______________________________

Finally, once you complete this book, I highly suggest you use this same process to evaluate your purpose for reading it and the actions you've taken to move your life to a better place.

If you find that you had difficulty stating a purpose for several of the resources you looked at in the audit, or you realize now that you haven't done much to put what you learned to use, you could be stuck in the Personal Development Vortex. It's not too late to implement some of the ideas you learned.

If you are unable to articulate your purpose for *this* book after reading this chapter the first time, that's ok. My suggestion is to reread the chapter again when you have a quiet moment. Sit with the information for a few minutes and then try the exercise again. This will help you move out of the "Vortex" and onto your purposeful path.

It's tempting to just move on with your life without giving these tools much thought. You're going to be inspired to find the next motivation text or TED Talk. But I promise you don't want to skim past what I've got on deck for you. Part 3 of this book is going to give you tools and methods that will equip you to break away portions of your pain while harnessing the parts that benefit you so you can truly live from a place of purpose.

This next section of the book can help you change your life. But again, you have to put what you learn into play.

Are you ready?

Let's get into it.

PART 3

PURPOSE

CHAPTER 11

LIVING ON PURPOSE

You've heard my pain, you've seen my progress, and as you turned from the last page to this one, there's a small part of you that hoped I'd greet you with a reassuring message, something like: "I'm cured. I'm free of my pain." As much as I'd love to deliver that message to you, I can't. It would be a bald-faced lie. The truth is this: the work—on yourself, your mindset, your beliefs, and your thoughts—never ends.

It's as constant as taking a shower or doing the laundry. If you go a few days without bathing, you and everyone around you will begin to catch a whiff of what you've been neglecting. If you go too long without doing a load or two of laundry, you'll be left naked and vulnerable to the world.

Finding a purpose within your pain works the same way. If you don't give it time, attention, and consistent effort, there will be highly unfavorable consequences.

I didn't snap my fingers after watching *The Secret* and become wealthy. I didn't wake up the day after the first personal development conference with an absence of fear or anxiety. My relationship and self-worth issues didn't vanish after meeting Lori. Personal growth and transformation are never a one-and-done proposition, and I'm a living testament to that. I am a far different man from the guy you met in the first part of this book, but I'm certainly not out of the woods yet.

I shower every day. I brush my teeth every day. And every day I commit to taking care of myself, my stories, and my willingness to press on despite the events I've experienced. Within my commitment, there are certain principles and practices I have incorporated into my life, allowing me to forgive who I was, stay centered in who I am, and stay focused on the person I'd like to become.

In the third and final part of this book, I'd like to share those tools with you.

The events of my past—and the stories I created about them—caused me a ton of pain.

New people, new environments, and new beliefs helped me make progress. The practices and principles we're about to get into have allowed progress to blossom into my life's purpose.

Not a day goes by that I don't think about my dad. I'm sure your pain is similarly ever present. It's hard for you to imagine a day that doesn't feel like it's suffocating you. But those days exist, I promise. My dad's memory used to haunt me, but now it just reminds me of all the life I've been lucky enough to live.

I've gone through my own version of hell to get here. But

the only reason I stay here—filled with gratitude, abundance, love, and peace—is because I consciously choose to work on myself every single day. As we wrap up this book, I'll give you a look at exactly what my daily commitment looks like.

Use all of the tools or a few, just promise me you'll commit to taking care of you. Do it consistently. Do it without apology. Do it with love.

Your purpose depends on it.

CHAPTER 12

FIND THE GIFT. DISCARD THE CURSE.

If you're reading this, you have gone through some shit at some point in your life.

How do I know? Well, because you're human. It's part of the deal. If you've gotten this far in the book, you know that I, too, have been to hell and back. But here's the rub: there has been a gift somewhere in your sea of suffering. Somewhere along the way, your adversity made you grow in a way that wouldn't have been possible otherwise. The circumstances and events of your past (or present) likely average out as a negative, but I can almost guarantee there is a speck of light in all that darkness.

It is possible to turn your pain into a fulfilling sense of purpose, find the gift, give it all your attention, and ignore everything else.

Take me for instance. Losing my dad when I was five, and then three more important men before I was twenty-five, left me depressed and desolate, but the experiences also convinced me I was going to have to work my ass off to learn what other boys my age learned from their dads. I didn't have a father to play catch with or someone to grab my rebounds during shooting practice. Knowing I lacked male role models turned me into a driven "no one will outwork me" athlete. I played with grit. I played with tenacity. Quite frankly, I played with anger.

And it worked. My pain and the perception that I had to work harder than everyone else transformed me into a great athlete, starring in football, basketball, and baseball. The field and the court were the only places I felt in control of how much I could win, since all I seemed to do was lose outside of my world of sports. If I wasn't playing, I felt lost. Consequently, I went to extreme lengths to make sure I was ready for game day. One particular injury exemplifies the insane measures I would take to keep playing.

When I was a junior in high school, I fell to the ground clutching my knee during a basketball game. It hurt badly, but all I wanted to do was get up and show everyone I was okay. That pattern has loomed large in my life since my youth, and athletics was no exception. No matter how much I was hurting, my life's experiences forced me to create the illusion that I was fine. Whether it was physical or emotional pain, I was gritting my teeth and powering through.

My knee, however, wasn't just a bump or bruise that I could walk off. I had completely torn my ACL and had some cartilage damage as well. The injury sidelines professional athletes for months, sometimes years. But not me. I couldn't be weak. I couldn't be hurt. I could not, would not, show pain or weakness.

Rather than taking the advice of the doctors who kept telling me I needed surgery, I played through the agony. I closed out the basketball season without missing a game.

Once the season wrapped up, anyone else would've taken a break and had the operation. Not me. Athletics was my savior from suffering, my outlet for anger. I needed to keep playing. I needed to get on the field. Baseball season was right around the corner and if I couldn't play, I would be lost. I had attached my identity to being an athlete—competition gave me a place where I could finally create some wins. The idea of not suiting up for the upcoming season on the diamond hurt my soul more than anything could hurt my knee. Jay the Athlete couldn't bear the weight of not competing.

So, what happened? I played an entire season of baseball with essentially no ACL in my knee, severe cartilage damage, and wave after wave of excruciating pain. Some days the knee swelled to the size of a cantaloupe, but I'd suck it up and limp out onto the field. I needed everyone to know I could keep showing up.

As the baseball season closed, I knew it was finally time to do something about my knee. But even as I accepted that surgery and recovery were inevitable, I had a new challenge on my hands. Football season was just four months away, and even though the usual recovery time for a surgery of that magnitude was nine months or so, I was hellbent on being ready for training camp. Guess what? On the first day of practice, I was ready to rock and roll.

How? I showed up for rehab more often than it was prescribed. I worked out like a maniac to make sure my body was in condition to perform. I rode my bike 50 miles a day to keep the muscles in my legs from atrophying. I didn't give myself the option of *not* being ready at the start of the season. There was no Plan B. Jay the Athlete wouldn't allow for such a circumstance.

I envisioned myself jogging onto the field for our first game. I could hear the roar of the crowd when my name came booming through the sound system after a play. I poured every ounce of my mental preparation into my physical rehabilitation. Every night as I drifted off to sleep, I'd see myself flying around the gridiron under the bright lights of Chelsey Field, our school's football stadium.

I beat the odds to get on the field opening night. I worked my ass off to be ready. I don't know if I would have been able to summon that level of courage and tenacity had I not gone through what I'd endured as a kid. All of the losses made me think I had to compensate for my lack of male leadership by busting my ass in the weight room and on the field. I never wanted to have the excuse that I couldn't hack it because I didn't have a dad to show me the way.

That drive was my gift, but it came with a curse. Fear lurked a layer or two beneath my drive. I didn't *want* to get back on the field for the love of the game. I *needed* to get back on the field so I could still be someone. Because if I wasn't Jay the Athlete, who the hell was I? Just Jay? That scared me more than anything. My athletic persona protected me from looking at my emotional and mental wounds and forced me to play through some physical infirmities as well. Problem is—sustaining that level of intensity was not possible. I was headed for burnout.

There had to be a better way.

• • •

I'm still driven today. That gift is here with me as I write these words at 4:15 a.m., well before the sun kisses the sky. But I've discarded the curse I used to pair with my hard work. I'm not writing this book, building my business, or changing the lives of my clients because I feel like I need to make up for a painful past. Instead of living out of fear, scared I won't be enough if I don't accomplish my goals, I'm living out of love. I honor the lives of those I've lost by doing the best I can with the life I have.

It's a subtle shift, but it will provide the momentum you need to transform your pain into your purpose. I wouldn't be as driven as I am if I hadn't lost my dad, but now I know that I don't need to carry the weight and agony of his death to complete the important work I feel called to do. I have found a gift within my pain and have discarded the part of it that no longer serves me.

Take a few minutes and think about all you've been through. Consider what parts of your story have made you stronger, more caring, or more resilient. Maybe you went through a nasty divorce, but you still shower your kids with love every day. Maybe you lost someone close to you, but their absence has inspired you to make them proud. Maybe you haven't talked to your family in years, but the disconnect has made you more independent.

I don't know your story of pain, but I promise you there is a gift somewhere within it. It has made you better in some way, even if you have not found it yet. Take a deep breath and listen to your intuition as you search for what you've gained from your past.

Once you find "your thing," give it all your attention. Honor it. Love it. Bring it with you as you move forward. Just because it has stemmed from a situation you'd rather forget doesn't mean it can't be used to make your life unforgettable. The key here is to part ways with the baggage you've added. You don't have to take it all with you, but you have every right to latch on to the beneficial parts.

My drive has served me well. It has taken me to heights I couldn't have imagined in my earlier life. I kept the drive—I abandoned the pain.

Take what you've earned and leave the rest behind. Keep the gift and know that you don't need to carry the curse with it.

CHAPTER 13

YOUR REPRESENTATIVE

Take a second and think about the first date you went on with your current partner (or maybe someone from your past). You were nervous and anxious, hoping that things would go well. You made sure to look your best, dusting off your best sports coat for the occasion or slipping into the little black dress you reserved for special moments. You spent the day thinking of funny stories to share or searching for intriguing answers to questions like, "What do you do for fun?" or "What's on your bucket list?" You did everything you could to present the absolute best version of yourself.

But the problem is, you never really showed up for that date, did you? The real you stayed home in sweats. The real you stayed tucked away and out of sight. We all know that first impressions are important, and you didn't think the real you would be compelling enough to create the spark you were seeking. So you sent your representative—your proxy.

You sent the cleaner, more polished version of you. You figured they weren't ready for the real, raw version of who you were:

- The person who had gone through something traumatic.
- The person who was still trying to heal.
- The person who had been burned by love before and was scared to death it would happen again.
- The person who saw a failure in the mirror.
- The person who had a hard time getting out of bed in the morning.
- The person who couldn't sleep at night.
- The person who didn't feel worthy of being on the date in the first place.

No, no, no. There's no way anyone could be ready to meet *that* you. So, you sent a polished replica of yourself to put on a show and to create the perfect perception.

Don't beat yourself up about it. Everyone has their representative. There's a good chance the person you were meeting on that first date sent their version as well. It's a game we all play when we meet someone new. We bring out the dog and pony show to create the illusion of having it all together. But you and I both know that no one has it all together. We all have our flaws, our weaknesses, and our baggage. Still, we insist on playing the game.

But the game can be dangerous. Your representative has a shelf life; he or she can't play your role forever. At some point, the real you has to emerge. Some trigger will bring you out of hiding; some event will pull off your mask. One way or the other, your authentic self will eventually show up to the party.

If you're lucky, the person you're with will love your flaws just as much as (if not more than) the facade you initially introduced. But most times, this is where relationships fall apart. The people who were on the first date don't match the people lurking behind their representatives. When things get real, the contrast between the real and the illusion creates a rift that can't be repaired. You felt safe hiding behind your mask; once it's gone (and it will eventually be removed), things get ugly.

Wouldn't it make more sense just to show up as the real you on the first date? You might think your representative is cooler, cuter, or funnier than you really are. Even if that's true, though, it doesn't matter. It would still be advantageous to bring your nerdy self and bad jokes along from the beginning. Why? Because it's not the big reveal of your insecurities, your weaknesses, or your flaws that turns people away. Your imperfections aren't the problem. It's the massive gap between who you really are and who you initially presented that makes things go sour. It's not the real you creating the chasm no valid relationship can cross—it's the disconnect.

Sending your proxy is not limited to the field of romance. You'll send him/her out to do business, to sweat at the gym, even to go on vacation. There are not very many places where your alternate persona does not appear first. Once the situation appears safe, you get "tagged in."

If you're looking for a prime example of representatives—yours and everyone else's—open up your phone. Instagram, Facebook, and every other social media platform give us all a grand stage to put on our best performance. Every post is perfectly crafted; every picture is captured through just the right filter. Everyone's trying to present their best self, but in reality, it's all a mirage—something that appears to be real, but really isn't. It's Representative 101.

But the thing is, especially in the context of finding a way through your pain, *at some point, you must retire your representative*. Send him on a permanent vacation. Book her a flight straight to the center of the Bermuda Triangle. Make him/her disappear.

Once your representative gets lost, the real you can step forward. Will it make you feel vulnerable? Absolutely. Will you be everyone's cup of tea? Probably not. But in your vulnerability, even though some people may not jibe with who you are or what you've gone through, you can connect with those who resonate with your story in a much deeper way.

One more time: human beings are an interpersonal species; we need each other. We need connection and community. If you keep sending your representative out into the world to try to create connection, you're doing yourself and the others you come across a disservice. From their standpoint, you're stringing them along and convincing them that they like who you are, when they don't even know you. From your perspective, you're giving yourself a false sense of hope that you're creating meaningful relationships. When "you" show yourself, the relationships crumble.

I had my own representative in life and in love for a long time. I was the tough guy, the one hardened by life. I didn't take shit from anyone and would stop at nothing to prove to everyone that I was going to make something of my life. The truth? I'm not all that tough. I have a big heart full of love and compassion for other people because I know they're all fighting battles similar to mine. I got lucky, though. Lori saw what was within me before I saw it within myself. She created a safe space for me to bring the real Jay out of the dark and into the light. I retired my representative and haven't looked back since.

When I let go of my representative, my life transformed. My life, my love, and my business flourished because I began showing up as the real me. I still feel exposed as I allow people to see who I am, knowing that I could be rejected or maligned for my imperfections. But more often than not, I'm embraced for my willingness to be myself.

My transparency has allowed me to bond with people whose experiences are similar to mine. We don't swap stories of misery; we inspire each other to keep going. My new approach allows me to have love in my life every single day. I couldn't have kept Lori by my side if I had continued operating as I was. Now I have an impact I would not have had when I was showing up without authenticity. People can't resonate with someone who isn't being real.

Letting go of my representative gave me real access to my purpose. The trauma of my life held me back for years, but once I allowed myself to open up and talk about it, the relief and release that followed accelerated my life in ways I struggle to explain.

To move past your pain, you must be willing to show it to others. Fighting the battle alone is depressing. Opening yourself and bringing other people on your journey will lift you up higher than you can imagine.

I know you think your representative is protecting you. But the safest thing you can do is to embrace who you are, what you've been through, and how events have affected your life. I said it in Part 1, and I'll repeat it here: Wounds need oxygen to heal. Your pain is no different. You need to let it out into the open air, to be true to it and who you are, and the rest will take care of itself. Your pain will mend; it will get better. And along the way, you'll connect with people in such a deep way that your purpose will fall into your lap.

Trust me. I'm still working on it every day.

CHAPTER 14

DEATH TO LIMITING BELIEFS

You know well by now how I endured the deaths of four people I loved dearly by the time I was twenty-five. The Grim Reaper picked on me for a quarter century and sent my world into a tailspin. Ironically, though, the thing that got me into this mess also pulled me out. Death cast a dark shadow over my life; then death pulled me back into the light.

You see, for me to close the door on my past, one more thing had to die: my old story. My beliefs about how little I was worth, how little I deserved, and how much of a victim I was needed to breathe their last breaths. I had to dig a grave for all of the momentum I'd given to those thoughts and beliefs and bury them like I had buried so many loved ones over the years.

If I wanted a chance at truly living, my limiting beliefs needed to go up in flames. Now that my life has evolved and I've moved past my pain and my story, I get to help my clients kill off their limiting beliefs as well. There is no better way to begin the process of elevating your life to the next level. In fact, it's where my process of coaching and serving others always begins.

Over the years, I've had the honor and privilege of leading seminars and retreats similar to the personal development conference that was the catalyst for so much change in my life. It gives me great joy to create an experience for others—to do for them what the conference did for me.

Most people show up with the intention of building themselves up and transforming their lives, which is admirable. But I quickly remind them that their paths to their versions of success will get a lot easier to navigate once they clear out the limiting beliefs positioned firmly in their way. Once I let my stories and limiting beliefs die off, my life accelerated in ways I didn't think were possible. Because I've seen the power of letting those old stories and beliefs die, I make that the starting point of my events. I teach clients and attendees to remove the beliefs, stories, and thoughts stubbornly standing in the way of a life well lived.

Everyone files in, eager to get started. I introduce myself, telling them a little bit about my life and how I got to where I am. Basically, I give them a three-minute version of this book. Once the pleasantries are out of the way, I direct their attention to a stack of Post-it notes and a strategically placed trash bin. I emphasize the importance of removing limiting beliefs. I also communicate that just talking and thinking about what needs to go won't drive the point home sufficiently.

I give everyone five minutes to scribble down as many limiting beliefs as they can think of. At first, no one writes anything. It's not exactly fun to write down where you're struggling in life, so the resistance is natural. Eventually, people start putting pen to Post-it, though, and they get a few ideas down. Some people can only think of one or two things, while others have ten to fifteen Post-its spread around the table in front of them. You might be thinking, "Only five minutes to write down everything that's standing in my way? There's no way I could come up with all of them in such a short time!" And you'd be right. No one gets all of their limitations down, but everyone comes up with something.

The point isn't to uncover every last thing that's holding you back; it's to practice thinking about what's on your mind and in your heart. Few people ever stop to see what's under the surface of their minds; they just accept whatever flows through their heads as fact. This little five-minute exercise gives people the opportunity to dust off the cobwebs and start looking around. It's like spending five minutes in the attic of your house. You haven't been there in a long time. You don't have any idea where to look for whatever it is you want. As you pick through the nonsense that's sat up there for decades, you invariably find something else buried in the corner or behind a box full of memories you haven't seen in a long time. Before you know it, you've discovered more than you originally planned.

Your limiting beliefs work the same way, my friend. I might ask you to spend five minutes looking around your mind, but you're bound to uncover some stuff that will leave you curious and itching to get back up there on your own time.

After the time is up, I step in and ask participants how they're feeling about what they wrote. Some are frustrated they couldn't think of anything. Some are frustrated that they came up with too many things. But in most cases, people are relieved to see their limiting beliefs on paper. When they record and read their own struggles, they realize what little power the limiting beliefs really have. After you let a limiting belief bounce around your brain for years, you feel it's in control. But when you see it on paper, maybe a centimeter tall, it doesn't seem so big and bad.

Everyone stares down at their limitations and sizes them up. I step back in to help them get rid of their beliefs once and for all. I tell them they've arrived at the easy part. "Take every single Post-it and every single limiting belief you've written down, rip it up, and throw it in the trash." The act of ripping the note in half symbolizes an individual's power to tear the thoughts and beliefs out of their minds. The act of tossing all the notes in the trash symbolizes where beliefs like that belong—in the garbage.

I really can't overstate the power of your beliefs; they can either build castles for you or prison bars around you. I had a few in my life that kept me locked in a life I kept desperately trying to escape. Due to the events of my childhood, I hung onto subconscious undertones like, "I'm not good enough," and "Bad things happen to me," for years on end. I felt like the death of my father was a punishment, as if I didn't deserve to have my dad. With each successive death, I believed I was destined for bad things. As time wore on, my assumptions became my reality.

The more I believed these notions, the more my life mirrored those beliefs. Bad things kept happening, and my circumstances made me feel inadequate. I was forever running away from the people, events, and situations that made me miserable. But the pieces of my physical world were not the enemy. My enemy was the poisonous beliefs running wild in my mind. They caused more unfortunate events to unfold—more damage in need of repair. If I wanted anything to change on the outside, I needed to shift some things on the inside first.

All personal breakthroughs begin with a change in beliefs.[7]

~ Tony Robbins

7 Tony Robbins, *Awaken The Giant Within*, (New York: Simon and Schuster, 2012), 100.

I had to part ways with my limiting beliefs. If you want to create a life that gives purpose to your pain, you must do the same. If you let limiting beliefs linger, they will continue to get in the way. I don't know what your limiting beliefs are, but I know you have them. How do I know? Because if you didn't, you would already have everything you desire. If you had no subconscious limitations, you wouldn't be reading this book. You'd be relaxing in Bali, feet in the sand, drink in your hand, and not a worry in the world. But here you are.

Take a look at the following list of commonly held beliefs and note which ones resonate with you. Don't think too much about it; just skim through and see which ones make you cringe, wince, or shudder.

- Money is hard to come by (it doesn't grow on trees).
- Rich people are bad.
- I'm not very funny.
- I'm not very smart.
- My sister (or brother) is better than me.
- My mom/dad likes my sibling more than me.
- That job's too hard for me.
- Only a guy/girl can do that job.
- All men/women are liars.
- All men/women are cheaters.
- I always get hurt in relationships.
- My boss is an asshole.

- I am not worthy of being loved.
- That person is so lucky.
- Nobody can be that happy.
- I'm not supposed to be successful.
- I'm not supposed to have money.
- It is what it is.

This list could continue, but we don't need to kill any more trees by recording every last one. The truth is, you probably already have an idea of what's standing in your way. Whether it comes from the list you just read or represents something that's been hovering in your mind for years, there's a good chance you have a sense of your own limitations. It may not be something you can consciously put your finger on, but you know something's there. Something is blocking your path. Before we get into the process of how to remove (and replace) these limiting beliefs, I need you to do something for me.

Take a deep breath and give yourself a break, because:

We learn our belief systems as very little children, and then we move through life creating experiences to match our beliefs.[8]

~ Louise Hay

---

8 Louise L. Hay, *You Can Heal Your Life Gift*, (Carlsbad, CA: Hay House, Inc., 1999), 22.

Kids are impressionable; you know that. They absorb the world around them and tend to act in accordance with what they're experiencing. If they see love, they show love. If they see hate, they figure out how to hate. If you drop an F-bomb in front of a three-year-old, he/she will repeat it back to you. Kids see, hear, and observe everything. There's no conscious filter weeding out false or disempowering things. They download everything into their little brains.

You and I were the same way. Moments destined to become memories imprinted things in our hearts and minds we have carried with us ever since.

You heard your grandparents talk negatively about money, so now you can't think about it without cringing. You watched your parents fight all the time, so you now believe love is a myth. You observed people complaining about how terrible their boss was, so you carry the belief that bad supervisors must be the norm. I saw death, destruction, depression, and despair, so I assumed they were as natural as anything else in life. Those traumas were as normal to me as going to an animated movie is for any other kid.

And then we do this very interesting thing: we carry those beliefs and ideas with us everywhere we go—until we see they're not serving us and we decide to remove them. You may not have made a conscious choice to pick up your limiting beliefs, but you have the chance to put them down now. That's a choice you can make—right now, today. If we don't choose to eradicate the beliefs from our psyche, we'll just find ourselves running into the same old problems.

As Dr. Wayne Dyer says, "The state of your life is nothing more than a reflection of the state of your mind."[9] If you've made up your mind that love is a myth, that rich people are bad, or that you just can't get into shape, you will find plenty of evidence and events to confirm those thoughts. Therefore, to change what you see happening around you, you have to give up the limiting beliefs you've been carrying.

But how? How can you part ways with something that has spent so much time in your psyche?

You do it by understanding the beliefs were likely built on fertile but faulty ground. Because these beliefs are formed in childhood, you have to go back to the place they were formed. Go back to the little kid who saw a nasty divorce, heard about how rich people are bad, or experienced sexual abuse, and let him know that he was dealt a rough hand. Let her know the truth: love doesn't have to fall apart, rich people can be generous, and the vast majority of adults keep their kids safe instead of taking advantage of them.

A smaller, more impressionable version of you misperceived how life really works. Now, it's your job to let him know (in love) that he was wrong. Dig up the root of the

---

9 Rev. Laurie Sue Brockway, "31 Motivational Quotes from Dr. Wayne Dyer," Huffington Post, updated December 7, 2017, https://www.huffpost.com/entry/-wayne-dyer_b_8066286.

problem and remove the weed at the source. Treating the issue at the surface level will not work.

I want to touch on one last thing about your limiting belief. You need to replace your beliefs (the ones blocking you) with empowering ones. Create a void where your old belief once was and give your mind the opportunity to fill it with something valuable and precious.

Once you remove what has been holding you back, you must fill the gap in your mind with something uplifting, inspirational, and empowering—something destined to move you forward. If you don't, you're just leaving room for your old limitations to slide back in and set up shop. It's like breaking up with someone, telling everyone it's over, and then letting your ex waltz back into your life when you feel lonely.

I don't want that for you, and you shouldn't want that for yourself.

So, how do you fill the void?

You use the truth that disproves the limiting belief you recently exterminated. Let's try out a few examples to illustrate what I mean.

Limiting Belief
All men are cheaters.
Truth
There are loyal, loving men in the world. Therefore, all men are not cheaters.
New Empowering Belief
There are loyal, loving men in the world, and I deserve to be with one of them.

Limiting Belief
My whole family is overweight, so I'm destined to be as well.
Truth
The right nutrition, mindset, and exercise regimen can overrule any genetic obstacle to weight loss.
New Empowering Belief
I am not a victim of my family's health history. I have the power to get in shape and to thrive.

Limiting Belief
Money is hard to come by.
Truth
There is currently $5 trillion in circulation worldwide.
New Empowering Belief
There is an abundance of money in the world, and I am worthy of my deserved chunk of it!

You get the idea. You fill the space between your ears with something true and empowering. The root of your limitations began in misperception; now it's your job to swap that out for an accurate and inspiring viewpoint.

The more limiting beliefs you trade for empowering ones, the more your results in life will reflect the diligent work you've done to change your mindset.

Your beliefs become your thoughts, Your thoughts become your words, Your words become your actions, Your actions become your habits, Your habits become your values, Your values become your destiny. [10]

~ Gandhi

What is the most important work you can do to turn your pain into purpose? Everything starts with belief. See the moments that caused and created the pain through a different, more empowering lens. It's up to you to provide the new prescription.

To end this chapter, I want to provide an exercise to rewire your belief system. Read through it step by step. Use it to

---

10 MindBodyGreen. n.d. "Gandhi: Your Beliefs Lead to Your Destiny." https://www.mindbodygreen.com/0-2957/Gandhi-Your-Beliefs-Lead-to-Your-Destiny.html

liberate yourself from what's been holding you back. If you take nothing else away from this book, carry the following exercise with you.

I use journal writing to practice the following exercise. Here is an example.

1. Acknowledge the limiting belief.

My limiting belief was that everyone I loved would be taken away, and I would experience more pain. Therefore, if I don't get close to people and allow myself to love, I will not experience more pain when they are gone.

2. Identify where the belief originated.

My limiting belief started when I was five after my father died in a head-on car accident. It was reinforced several times by the deaths of others close to me.

3. Challenge the belief.

There is no solid evidence that my belief is true. Yes, I experienced the loss of people very close to me, but the number of people who have lived and who are living in my life far exceeds the number I have lost.

4. Declare the belief to be a false belief.

I created this belief when I was five years old, and I have allowed it to control me for far too long. I know I created it. Therefore, I can destroy it and create a new belief around the same event.

5. Replace this limiting belief with a new and empowering truth.
Life happens for me, not to me. I know and believe this to be my truth. I believe the events of my life, even the painful ones, have created the person I am today. Without these events, I would not be able to help other people overcome their pain. As crazy as it may sound, I am grateful for my life—all of it.

6. Reinforce your new belief with your new powerful story.
Because of my experiences and battles with pain, I am now able to help others overcome their tragedies. This is my life's purpose, and I am grateful for the ability to help others live happier, more fulfilling lives.

EXERCISE

Remember, this is not a one-time quick fix. You need to work through this process consistently until you have created new neural pathways and beliefs that magnify your new powerful, positive life.

1. Acknowledge the limiting belief. This is going to require you to be brutally honest with yourself.

____

____

____

____

____

2. Identify where the limiting belief originated so you can understand why it has power over you.

____

____

____

____

____

3. Challenge the limiting belief. This will help you see that the belief is not necessary and will empower you to remove it from your life.

____

____

____

____

____

4. Declare your old belief to be false and acknowledge you have the ability to remove it from your life.

____

____

____

____

____

5. Replace the limiting belief with a new and empowering truth about your life. The *only* way to remove a limiting belief is to replace it with another, overpowering one.

____

____

____

____

____

6. Reinforce your new belief with your new, powerful story.

____

____

____

____

____

As I stated above, following these steps and completing this exercise once is awesome and will help you, but it won't be good enough to eradicate your limiting beliefs forever. Just as going to the gym once won't give you big biceps, doing the limiting belief work once won't dispel the beliefs you've held for years.

But with repetitive daily/weekly practice, you can replace your old thoughts of limitation with new powerful thoughts of growth and happiness.

Commit to adding these and all the exercises in this book to your weekly plan. I still use every one of these exercises to this day. That's how I know they work.

CHAPTER 15

PERCEPTION VERSUS REALITY

We don't see things as they are, we see them as we are.

~ Anais Nin, Seduction of the Minotaur

Truth is relative, and when your relationship with the world has been a painful one, your perception of what's real and what's not gets pretty screwed up. When you've gone through hard times, the lens of your environment gets clouded by the rocky circumstances of your world. The lines between fact and fiction get blurred by your experience, and you begin to believe what was true for you is true for everyone.

My conscious mind pretty much woke up at five years old when we learned about Dad's death. I honestly don't remember much of anything before that day in 1980, so my first memory was of suffocating pain. At the moment I heard the news about my father, life handed me a smudged lens. I viewed the world through that faulty lens for a long time. For what feels like forever, I only saw pain. I would find the negative in any situation. I pointed out problems to all the happy-go-lucky optimists in any circumstance. I did not have some super-sensitive sixth sense to predict danger; all I saw was pain every time I opened my eyes. My blinders made me lock in on the bad stuff. I was laser focused on all the ways things could go wrong. I had no energy for what might go well.

That's what painful moments do to all of us. Our difficult experiences sink their teeth into our psyches and force us to believe that our experiences represent absolute truth when in reality we just had the misfortune of being in a bad situation or circumstance. What I went through isn't normal, and your dance with pain likely isn't either. But our brains like to tell us not only to trust in the "normalcy" of those moments, but also to expect more to come our way. And wouldn't you know it, we get what we expect. We see more of what we believe to be normal, and the cycle repeats itself until we consciously decide to interrupt the thought pattern.

I saw more and more pain around me as the years wore on, and I can make a fair assumption that you have as well. When pain presses on your heart and soul, it's hard to look out at the world and see anything different. In fact, it's damn near impossible. But again, it's because we don't see things as they are; we see them as we are. When we're drowning in pain and suffering, the world seems to overflow with more of the same.

That's why it's imperative for you to shift your energy

from changing your circumstances to improving who you are. If you ever want to find a true purpose from all of the pain you've been through, this is the only way.

The notion of changing my emphasis is what woke me up. Once I was introduced to it—and truly understood what the hell it meant—I stopped trying to change the world outside of myself and put all of my energy into shifting my perceptions and perspectives. For the first time, I took a step back and looked at what else was present in my life besides the pain hogging the spotlight. I finally stepped into a different perspective and found my perception of the events of my life slowly starting to shift.

Where I once saw pain, I now saw strength. I could finally see how strong and resilient I had become.

I replaced a sense of loss with an understanding of legacy. Rather than observing the death of my dad as a tragic and hopeless loss, I recognized an opportunity to honor his memory through raising the standards of my own life.

The suffering I had endured now seemed voluntary instead of inevitable and mandatory. It was natural to grieve when my loved ones passed, but there was no reason to remain in a state of mourning for decades.

The more that I worked on myself in the present—generating inner strength, garnering a sense of my legacy, and taking responsibility for my own life—the more I could look back and see those qualities in my younger self. The events themselves never changed, but as I changed, I could see those pain-filled memories in a different light.

My new perception allowed me to heal a lot of old wounds, but it also helped me reframe negative experiences in real time as I experienced them. Once I understood the power of my perception, I realized I could maneuver around or through every obstacle I encountered. I could choose a perception that would empower me instead of defeat me.

Through the course of doing the work for myself, I developed a reframing technique I'm happy to share with you. You can use it as you reflect on your past or to iron out any present difficulty. Either way, it will give you a new perspective and will shift your point of view so you can find meaning and rewrite the story about the event in question.

POSITIVE REFRAMING TECHNIQUE

First and foremost, construct an honest account of what happened. Notice that I said *honest*. Remove the drama and your (probably skewed) story of what happened and seek the facts. While it may sound too simple, this step in the process is *essential*. If you want to change the way you see the event you're working through, you must first step away from your original position. Visualize your memory of it and write it all down. See all the facts and figures laid out in front of you. If you notice something emotionally charged, erase it. There's a good chance that if you are remembering how you felt or what emotions came up, you're still living in your story. Our goal is to begin to live without it.

Once you've got an idea of what went down, ask yourself these powerful (and potentially triggering) questions:

- How is this positive for me?
- How am I benefiting from this event?

Did you feel a tinge of resistance just now? You may have even cussed me out in your head after reading those all-important inquiries.

"How in the world can I find something positive in this mess of a situation, Jay? Are you out of your mind?"

No, I'm not out of my mind. But you are very much in yours. You're in your head, trying to find one good reason you went through this event. I need you to sink into your heart and your soul. Deep within you there lies legitimate answers to the questions. There is something good that came from the event you experienced. Remember, you need to find the gift within the curse. You need to search for something positive amid what you've previously seen as an ocean of negativity.

Once you find that glimmer of hope, that sliver of positivity, open your mind back up and visualize the situation again. At the beginning of this exercise, I asked you to remove your story and decrease the drama from what you were seeing. I wanted the slate to be blank so you could only see facts.

This time, however, I want you to insert your positive spin on the event as it's happening in your mind's eye. I want you to highlight and honor the good in the moment, slowly creating an event that feels nothing like it did when you experienced it in real time. What you focus on expands, so bringing a perspective of positivity to the scene will shed light on a moment once filled only with darkness.

Then there's the grand finale, the moment where you take what you've seen and extract a lesson from the experience. From the beginning of this exercise to its conclusion, pick out what you've learned. If you can acknowledge the power you've gotten from this new perspective, you can more readily bring the same information to similar experiences moving forward. That way, you can sidestep events that might get you stuck in the future. Consider three examples:

If you looked back on your painful moment and saw that someone who hurt you was in pain themselves, you can find more compassion for the next person who lashes out at you.

If you looked back and saw that your adversity gave you strength and resolve, you can be grateful for any obstacles you may face on your path, since you know they will only make you better.

If you looked back and were reminded that what seems devastating in the moment never has to be, you can approach any breakup, lay off, or rough patch with the understanding it won't be the death of you.

Once you've extracted the lesson, ponder how you can apply it to all the major areas of your life. How can compassion help your career? How can finding gratitude for your obstacles assist in your relationships? How can an understanding of impermanence support your spiritual pursuits? The more holistic you can make your lesson, the better. It will permeate your life and become a subconscious certainty rather than a fleeting, conscious thought.

I've used this exercise so much it has become second nature to me. It has not only healed parts of my past, but it has also helped me navigate everything causing resistance in the here and now. Use the following template to work it out for yourself. It will change your life. I promise.

1. What happened? Remember to be honest with your account. No dramatics allowed.

____

____

____

____

____

2. Why was this positive? Write down all the positives you can extract from the situation.

____

____

____

3. What am I supposed to learn from this situation? Write down the lesson you've extracted.

4. How can I apply this lesson to the following areas of my life?

My Relationships:

My Money or Work:

My Health:

My Spirituality:

Your ability to reframe situations past and present will be one of your greatest tools as you move forward to create your new story.

I now use this tool on a daily basis without even thinking about it. Remember, you don't see the world as it is, you see the world as you are. Your ability to positively reframe situations that would typically throw you into a negative spiral will quickly become your secret weapon for navigating life with a smile on your face.

CHAPTER 16

STACKING MOMENTUM

If you've known me prior to reading this book, you probably know how much value I place on the quality of people in a support system; you know I call it your Circle of Success. Ever since I met Lori and committed to creating a better life for myself, I've realized how important it is to keep people around who challenge me. If no one is pushing me out of my comfort zone, I'll just stay put. I am very intentional about the people I give my time and energy to, and I invest in coaches, programs, and masterminds to support my continual growth.

One person I'm privileged to call a mentor is none other than Ed Mylett, uber-successful businessman and host of the #MaxOut YouTube channel. I have learned a ton from Ed, but one of the biggest lessons he's handed down to me can be summed up by the following:

> *Momentum is the magic multiplier that can create everything you desire if you harness it, pay attention to it, and stack upon it.*

There is nothing quite like the feeling of momentum. Like a snowball rolling downhill, just a little bit of movement can eventually translate to a powerful force once things start moving. An object's momentum doesn't begin as a massive, unstoppable force. It starts as a small thing that keeps picking up size and/or speed the more it continues down its path.

To create momentum in your life, you first need to take action. You have to act toward the things you desire. It has to start small, but over time and with continuous effort, it can grow into something you can't imagine right now. If you've been (or currently are) in pain, all you want is the opposite. You do not want to hurt anymore. If you're sad, you want to feel happy. If you're broken, you want to feel whole. If you're hurting, you want to feel healed.

Understand that building momentum toward what you want starts with the smallest of steps, one that will most likely barely move the needle. Trust it. Over time, if you keep taking small steps, you will create downhill momentum that will accelerate you toward the life you desire.

A journey of a thousand miles begins with the first step.[11]

~ Lao-Tzu

11 Tao Te Ching - Lao Tzu - chapter 64, https://www.wussu.com/laotzu/laotzu64.html

Momentum can be a flowing force in your life, but you can never create it without moving your butt off the starting line. Standing still never translates to the powerful movement of momentum.

You might be thinking, "I don't know, Jay. This whole momentum thing sounds great. But I don't even know what that would feel like. I've never experienced it myself."

Once again, I call bullshit! At some point in time, you've had the strong winds of momentum at your back, but maybe you were headed down the wrong path. The tricky thing about momentum is it can work in both directions. It can allow you to move swiftly in a positive direction, giving you the opportunity to accomplish your goals. That's the easy one to sense. But momentum can also apply negative movement in your life. You can find yourself in the middle of a downward spiral of momentum, moving fast toward a life you absolutely don't want.

Momentum doesn't discriminate. If you take small action steps toward the positive life you crave, the consistent effort will eventually translate into a powerful headwind of energy pushing you toward your dream life. By contrast, if you consciously or unconsciously believe, think, and act within a negative frame of mind, you'll find yourself trying to escape the quicksand of a life you dread.

You get to choose which way momentum carries you. If you've found yourself moving in an unfavorable direction, it's never too late to change course. Problem is, if you want to escape the downward spiral negative momentum creates, you have to work twice as hard to right the ship.

No one's immune to the sinkhole of negative self-talk or unfortunate circumstances. I've certainly been there before. But knowing what I know now, I do everything in my power to get things back on track so I can use the momentum in my life to move me toward my goals rather than away from them. Let me fill you in on what has worked for me.

MOMENTUM U-TURN

First and foremost, if you sense your thoughts, beliefs, attitude, and actions have been favoring the negative side of the spectrum, it's imperative to bring things to a halt as quickly as possible.

The longer you wait, the more momentum you'll accumulate toward an undesirable destination. What might seem like petty pessimism and silly cynicism right now compounds over time to bring on anger, frustration, and depression. Have compassion for yourself; decide to change your direction right now. If you continue on the negative road, your life will only deteriorate.

When I find myself headed in the wrong emotional and energetic direction, I go all in on action. Once I sense something's off, I double down on all of my habits to generate my most uplifting and empowering emotional states:

Instead of taking the time to note what I'm grateful for once a day, I sit down three times a day to say thank you to the Universe.

Instead of reaching out and encouraging three people in my circle, I message ten.

Instead of getting one workout in, I add a hike with Lori or a walk with our dog, Rudy.

I maximize all the actions I know will ignite my best self and use them to pivot the position of my momentum.

After a day or two of massive action, I find myself relieved of the suffocating funk. Just like that, the tide turns back in my favor and I'm cruising along.

Sounds simple, right? Well, it is. I know you want to make it complicated. You want the process of shaking off your funk to take twelve steps, involve spending money you don't have, and require investing time in something you cannot possible squeeze into your schedule. You want it to be hard so it will be easy to quit. But I make it easy so it becomes very difficult to give up. All it takes is focused, intentional action on meaningful things in your life. Once you lock in on them, you'll be back on the positive momentum train.

Once you're back on the right track, allowing your momentum to push you forward instead of backward, maximize it by stacking wins along the way. There are so many people who are fighting to make their lives better but won't allow themselves to celebrate anything until they've reached certain milestones. When it comes to the game of momentum, you don't want to wait long. If you put it off until you've reached some arbitrary checkpoint, you may run out of juice on the way.

Instead, celebrate everything along the route. Pat yourself on the back when you take the necessary small action steps. Have a champagne toast when you take the big, scary leaps forward. Just be sure to honor and celebrate your progress.

How do the celebrations help? Because when you keep reminding your mind, body, and soul that you are moving in the right direction, it will feel like a strong wind at your back, carrying you forward. It will add to the energy you've built and all your accumulated results because the small festivities will make you more aware of your successes in every step of the process.

If you want to transfigure your pain into purpose, harnessing some momentum is crucial. I'd be willing to bet that you've experienced your fair share of negative momentum. Whatever triggered it does not matter, whether large or small. The magnitude is not important.

The essential issue is understanding that one instance—one falling domino—led to a life spiraling out of control. Perhaps you felt that bad luck was following you. In truth, you were feeling the pull of negative momentum—it was dragging you farther along the path of despair.

It's time for you to choose the first step in the opposite direction. To stack momentum in your life, you must find the courage and permission to bring it back to a path destined to serve you best. Move swiftly. Be strong. I'm happy to give you permission, and I hope you can find the inner courage to build momentum toward your best self.

CHAPTER 17

MINDFULTATION

I've spent most of my life in darkness. That's what pain really is, isn't it? Just a lonely cave of darkness with little to no light penetrating the soul-crushing gloom and doom. From the moment the five-year-old me ran through the door of our house to see why a state trooper was there until I was about thirty, all I knew was darkness.

But once I woke up to what my life could be like and chose a different path than the one of massive pain and negative momentum, something weird happened—something I didn't expect. As I began to shift and transform my life, I assumed I would simply shed everything that had been weighing me down and rise up to a new standard of living. Boy, was I wrong!

To be clear, I experienced a lot more joy, gratitude, and abundance in my life as a result of bettering myself and my mindset. But a lot of the demons I buried well before then decided to come out and play.

There's a certain defense mechanism we all have when we're in pain. To get on with our lives as normally as possible, we tend to smother any memories or emotions that might trigger the pain we have tucked deep within us. I had stowed away a lot of thoughts and moments of my past to avoid dealing with them.

As I opened myself up to Lori, growing my business, and living my best life possible, I also opened up a can of worms. I hoped I would never see the "squiggly things" again, but to rise above the way I was living, I needed to address every part of my identity—the things binding me to my past life. All the trauma from my childhood. All the experiences I had as a result of the deaths I had witnessed. Every failed relationship, every missed opportunity, and every morning I didn't get out of bed came rushing back into my consciousness.

It was scary as shit. It made me want to sprint back into my cave of darkness. The dark and lonely cavern felt safer than the vulnerability of addressing all of the emotions I had successfully suffocated for years. But at the same time, I knew I had to process all of those emotions and my resistance to feeling them if I wanted to step into a life where I could be, do, and have anything I wanted. I had to face the fear of looking all of the painful memories in the eye. I had to deal with all of them if I ever wanted to build and to sustain the life I was looking to create.

In those moments of fear, I knew I needed to come up with something that would allow me to process those emotions. I needed a tool through which to experience how I was feeling (for the first time in a long time) in a healthy and productive way.

"Mindfultation" was born.

No, you didn't read that wrong. Although I recognize the massive benefits of meditation, sitting quietly with my legs crossed while humming "Ommm" isn't my jam. Sitting still and asking my brain to quiet itself is like asking a Kardashian to go twenty-four hours without taking a selfie. It's just not going to happen. But again, since I know meditation is such a useful tool, I wasn't ready to dismiss it entirely. I just needed to find a way to do it my way. I began to incorporate mindfultation into my daily routine, and it's been a godsend. I use it more now than I did back when I came up with it because I've seen how much value it has brought to my life. It is a non-negotiable for me, allowing me to sit with what I'm thinking and feeling so I can start my day as centered as possible.

"All right, Jay. What the hell is this mindfultation stuff and how does it work?"

I thought you'd never ask.

First, I find a quiet space with no distractions. You don't have to make this a difficult part of the process. I've seen people punk themselves out of trying this routine because they couldn't find a perfectly peaceful place to engage. So, I'm addressing it now before we get too far ahead of ourselves. There is no perfect spot. Just find somewhere quiet and relax. To be completely honest, sometimes I do this in my office, at my studio, or even just sitting by the pool in my backyard. The only requirement is peace and quiet, got it?

Once I've sequestered myself and have some space to get down to business, I pull out my journal and do a brain dump. A brain dump is exactly what it sounds like. Your mission is simply to let your mind leak onto the page without judgment or hesitation. You're not trying to write a college dissertation or romantic poetry. The only goal is to open up and see what comes spilling out. Some of the things I write down are straight up nonsense, but once I start letting it flow, I eventually come back to an issue I need to deal with or a goal I want to accomplish. I'm not trying to directly solve any problems right then and there. I'm simply looking for what's going on between my ears so I have all the emotional and energetic information I need to make sound decisions about what's currently in my life.

After I've put some words to the workings of my mind, I read back through whatever I wrote. I make note of anything that jumps off the page at me and bookmark it for later consideration. Sometimes the revelations are *huge* and other times they're basic and routine. I don't spend any time judging the magnitude of my thoughts each morning, though. I simply work with whatever comes out and do my best with it.

Then comes the mindful piece of mindfultation. I sit quietly and think about what came out in the process. I ponder my thoughts. I look for clarity on decisions I need to make or conversations I need to have. It's as if I'm seeing my own thoughts as a third party and I'm trying to counsel myself on what it all means. When I enter into this phase of the process,

I've actually found that doodling is an awesome way to deepen the connection with my thoughts. It gives my body something physical and mindless to do, therefore freeing up more mental capacity for me to explore the inner workings of my thoughts. Just so you don't think I'm batshit crazy for taking this detour into "Doodleland," check out the following endorsements of doodling from these well-respected voices:

- *Doodles come straight from the Unconscious. That's partly why they work.*[12]
  ~ Steven Pressfield, author of *The War of Art*

- *To doodle is not to waste time or to be distracted. Instead, doodling is a powerful technique people use around the world to help themselves THINK. As scientists, innovators and even presidents know, doodling is a precursor to and a catalyst for deep intellectual and creative breakthroughs.*[13]
  ~ Sunni Brown, author of *The Doodle Revolution: Unlock the Power to Think Differently*

---

12 Steven Pressfield, *The War of Art*, Self-published, 2012.

13 Sunni Brown, *The Doodle Revolution: Unlock the Power to Think Differently*, (New York: Portfolio – Penguin, 2014).

Once I've doodled a bit and sat with my thoughts for a while, I revert to journaling mode and write down anything that feels clearer after letting it bubble in my mind for a while. This is the part of the process where I gain extreme clarity and answers to the questions I may have brought to the table at the beginning. I jot down any nuggets that come through powerfully and purposefully, then smile and go about my day knowing whatever presented itself to me during mindfultation will somehow serve me in the day ahead. It always does, and I promise if you use this practice with intention, what you find in this quiet time will serve you, as well.

In the beginning you will judge yourself and your thoughts, and you may doubt whether the process is even doing anything. You will question if you should stick with it or not. This is all very normal. It's called a practice for a reason; you need to attempt it more than a handful of times before you start to see improvement and results. Just trust and believe that the time spent in the mental trenches is worthwhile and that your commitment to yourself in this way will bring you growth and transformation.

I often indulge in this practice twice a day or more. The more you exercise the mental muscles that quiet the noise of your daily life, the more you will find the clarity you seek as you transform your pain into a meaningful purpose.

Now it's your turn to work through the process.

I want you to use the technique I have just taught you and

complete the exercise below.

Remember, this is a daily practice, and the more you do it, the more valuable it will become. You will need to work through this process consistently until you have created a new powerful level of mindfulness and appreciation.

1. The "Brain Dump." Write down all the things currently floating around in your thoughts. Remember, don't judge, just write.

____

____

____

____

____

____

____

____

2. Make a mental note of all the nuggets or thoughts needing more clarity. I've given you some space here to write because when you first begin this practice, you might need to rewrite or make notes on the *big* thoughts.

3. Now it's time to sit quietly with your thoughts. Be open to receive, and let your mind guide you to the clarity and answers. Use doodling to get even deeper into your subconscious mind.

4. It's journal time again. Write down anything that came to you during your quiet time of mindfulness. Don't judge your thoughts. Sometimes they won't make sense initially but in a few hours or a few days, an *aha* will hit you like a ton of bricks. Reminder: You must be open to receive. If you don't believe, you can't receive.

If practiced and applied daily, your mindfultation sessions will become a sacred part of your day because they are going to bring you the clarity you need to navigate the world with peace and passion.

I urge you to make time for this practice, as I know it's been a pivotal part of my success journey.

When we are clear-minded, decisions become easy, and adversity turns into opportunity.

CHAPTER 18

YOUR CIRCLE OF SUCCESS ISN'T GOOD ENOUGH

You know I'm big on surrounding myself with people who inspire me to do more and challenge me to rise to the occasion. Having a Circle of Success is one of my core pillars of coaching. I constantly remind my clients that they are who they hang out with the most.

- If you hang around five idiots, you'll be the sixth.
- If you hang around five intelligent people, you'll be the sixth.
- If you hang around five millionaires, you'll be the sixth.
- If you hang around five confident people, you'll be the sixth.
- If you hang around five broke people, you'll be the sixth.

Your proximity to people is important, because *you become who you spend your time with*. In the context of pain, suffering, and all the despair I experienced in my childhood, the circle of people I surrounded myself with kept me in the emotional state I so desperately wanted to escape. My family and friends who were close to my dad were grieving in their own ways. Since I was a kid, I couldn't do anything but sit and sulk with them. It wasn't their fault by any means, as they all dealt with the loss in their own way. But being in close proximity to such a low emotional state made it even more difficult for me to find my way to the light.

Consider those you've been close to since your experience of pain. Have they been helping you heal or keeping you stuck? It's an important question to chew on but do so without judgment. Observe your surroundings as objectively as possible and see if you need to break away from the crowd that constantly reminds you of where you've been and what you've gone through. When I moved from my hometown to join Lori in California, the new atmosphere and environment made my growth exponential. I didn't have the physical and personal reminders of my past, so I was able to rise above them with relative ease.

But the point of this chapter isn't to preach the importance of your circle. If you follow me on social media or have read my other books, you've already heard the speech. The point I want to drive home here is that having a Circle of Success is only the first step. Surrounding yourself with supportive people is just the beginning.

Once you've found a tribe in line with what you want to create in your life, it's imperative for you to integrate what these powerful people might be modeling. Just being around successful people isn't good enough. As with anything else, you can't learn through osmosis. This is what I mean when I say your circle by itself isn't good enough. It's not that you don't have good people in your life—you simply need to embrace all they have to offer in an actionable way.

If you're just sitting back and observing your friends doing great things, you're doing about as much as someone who simply reads books for knowledge but never does anything with the information. Watch the amazing people rise above their circumstances and then follow suit. Observe them act to lose their stubborn weight and then join them at the gym. Take note as they hire a coach and start shaking off the shackles of their past. Then hire that coach to help you do the same. *Building* your Circle of Success is crucial but *imitating* those powerful people is the difference between finding purpose in your pain or staying stuck in it.

I'll be completely honest with you: this book wouldn't exist if I hadn't followed the advice I'm giving you here. A few years back, I had an itch to write my first book, *The Overweight Mind*, but kept spinning my wheels on it. Then I looked around at some of the people in my Circle of Success and noticed they were publishing books and inspiring others through what they had to say. I started asking those people for advice on how to write the damn thing, how to get it published, edited, the whole nine yards. Had I not acted and followed the example of those in my circle, I would never have written my first book. If I hadn't seen the impact I could have with *The Overweight Mind*, I doubt I would have pursued my passion for the project you're currently enjoying.

Get yourself in the same room with inspirational people, then follow their lead.

Let's take inventory and set up action steps you can take to use the strengths of the people in your Circle of Success.

List four members of your Circle of Success and one person who is currently not in your circle but needs to be for you to step to the next level. You might not even know the fifth person at this moment, but you know what attributes they possess that will help you learn and grow from them.

Current member of your Circle of Success:

Member 1
Name:
Strengths:
Habits You Will Model:

Member 2
Name:
Strengths:
Habits You Will Model:

Member 3
Name:
Strengths:
Habits You Will Model:

Member 4
Name:
Strengths:
Habits You Will Model:

Member 5
The Person You Need (if you don't currently know them, give them a made-up name for the time being)

Name:
Strengths:
Habits You Will Model:

I personally do a quarterly audit of my Circle of Success, not because I am always looking to replace people but because I know the human tendency to get comfortable, to settle for average when excellent should be our standard.

During my audit, I also do a self-evaluation. How am I showing up for my circle? Your Circle of Success is a two-way street. You can't expect from others what you aren't willing to give yourself.

If cultivated and appropriately grown, your Circle of Success will be one of your most substantial assets as you move into your new story of growth and development.

CHAPTER 19

VISUALIZATION

The book in your hand has been written a thousand times over. It's not that I rattled through numerous rough drafts before writing one worthy of publishing; I've simply seen these words on the movie screen of my mind more times than I can count. I have visualized everything coming together so this message would find the people it was meant for, creating a ripple effect of purpose and positivity in the world. Right now, you are experiencing the moment my thoughts became a reality. Pretty cool, right? I'm honored to have you here as I make my visual dreams a very real experience.

The practice of visualization is nothing new, but I promise this approach will maximize everything you've learned so far. I'm not blowing smoke up your ass when I tell you that this book is the product of many mornings and nights spent visualizing this exact message and platform in my mind. If you're looking for evidence to show the actualization of visualizing, you're reading it right now.

In its most basic form, visualization is simply creating a mental image in your mind. Anyone who has a pulse has visualized something; it's just a matter of how intentional they have been about the image they've created. As a kid, you undoubtedly pictured what Christmas morning would be like as Santa's arrival drew nearer. You've likely created a mental movie about your wedding day or what having a kid would be like. We've all drifted into daydream-land and found ourselves imagining something exciting.

But when you hear about visualization in the culture of personal development, it has less to do with daydreaming about a single event and more to do with manifesting your greatest successes. So, how can you harness the power of visualization instead of just experiencing it passively and with limited results? To answer that question, I'm going to put my lab coat on and drop a little science on you. Let's get nerdy, shall we?

HABITUALIZING WHAT YOU VISUALIZE

Like me, you have habitual behaviors. Brushing your teeth, driving your car, and reading without having to think of every letter and syllable's pronunciation are just a few behaviors you probably do on autopilot. That's kind of the point, though. Habits are just patterns of behavior you've repeated, locked into your subconscious mind, and run automatically. You want to know why you can't bring a visualization to life? It's because you don't do it often enough. In other words, you haven't made it a habitual practice.

Let's say you have a heap of debt. You want to get rid of it. You have heard that visualizing the result of being debt-free can help the process, so for a week, you sit with the vision and dream about what solvency would be like. After a week or two, you still have debt. You give up the idea because it seems ludicrous.

Your visualization is not the problem. You simply did not give the routine enough time to become habitual. You bailed on the idea before your mind "got in the flow." Any energetic progress you made fell flat.

You want your grandest vision to show up for you? You have to lead the way and show up for it. Repeatedly. I visualize my goals and desires six times a day at minimum. In moments when my mind is free to wander, I rein it in and focus on what I want to create in my life. When I'm brushing my teeth, when I'm driving in the car, and when

I'm in the shower, I have my mind zeroing in on all my goals and aspirations.

The habitual nature of how often I *look at and think about* what I want is *why I keep getting* what I want. It's not because I'm special or have some sort of spiritual superpower. I just show up for practice more often than most.

You may be thinking, "But, Jay, I don't have time to sit down and think about all of this stuff as often as you do." Again, I'm going to (lovingly) call bullshit. You do have time, you're just misusing it because your priorities and purpose are misaligned. Get clear on what you truly desire out of life and you'll find the time.

You see, just like momentum, visualization doesn't play favorites. People on both sides reap the results. In my former life, I took in a bountiful harvest from the seeds of negative visualization I sowed everywhere in my life. People who repeatedly visualize the worst-case scenario often see it manifested. When we worry all the time, bad stuff happens. The bad things have nothing to do with bad luck—nothing to do with God being angry. We've simply imaged the most terrible possibilities until they eventuate in the most terrible probabilities.

A vision that becomes habitual has a better chance of becoming reality. Just like any other habit you have, the more you partake in the practice, the easier it becomes. It shifts the mental energy from the conscious mind to the subconscious mind, making the action more and more automatic. When was the last time you drove to the grocery store and had a difficult time remembering how to steer, put your blinkers on, or brake at every red light? It's been a while since you've had to turn your brain on to drive, so I'm sure it was a pretty simple journey. You want that level of ease for your vision. You want it to become so habitual that your mind just knows what to do and what images to create. The more work you put into the visualization ritual, the easier it will be for your best life to find its way to you.

Showing up to the experience makes it easier to find a more precise image of what you want, but what causes that image to come to life?

RETICULAR ACTIVATING SYSTEM

At the stem of your brain you have this little thing called the Reticular Activating System, or RAS.[14] It's a diffuse network of nerves that essentially serves as your brain's filtration system. When you look around a room, how many things can you see? How many things can you hear? What can you touch? Your senses are always abuzz trying to identify what's going on around you. You might think there's not much for your senses to identify, but you'd be wrong.

At any given moment, you are swimming through an ocean of sensory information. There are innumerable things for your senses to absorb, each one screaming to your brain, "Look at me! Listen to me. Smell me!" If all that information made its way in, your brain would essentially curl into the fetal position.

That's where your RAS comes in. Rather than letting all of the stimuli flow into your brain, your RAS filters out the minutiae and only lets through what matters. This is why—no matter how loud it is around you—hearing someone call your name will cut through everything else as clear as day. Your name is obviously important to you, so your RAS lets that be the first thing your brain picks out of the noise.

---

14 Dean Bokhari, "The Power of Focusing on What You Want (How Your Brain's Reticular Activating System Functions in Your Favor)," *Meaningfulhq.com* (blog), accessed June 6, 2019. https://www.meaningfulhq.com/reticular-activating-system-function.html.

Your RAS is also responsible for that strange experience when you learn something new and then begin seeing it and hearing about it everywhere you go. Whether it is a new word or an amazing TV show, once your RAS has been put on notice (once it's on alert there is something of importance), it allows you to realize it more and more often. So, if the next book you read mentions this whole Reticular Activating System, you'll know why. Now that it's been placed in your awareness, you'll begin seeing more and more about it.

For the purpose of visualization then, your RAS plays a key role in bringing your vision to life. Since its function is to give your brain more of what's important to you, a repeated practice of visualization will begin to reprogram this magnificent filtering system to bring more and more amazing things into your awareness. Think of your RAS as a bouncer. Your repeated imagining of the life of your dreams simply informs it about who's allowed to come into the party.

If you visualize a healthy and fit body, you're communicating to your RAS that it is important to you. All of a sudden you begin seeing ads for new gyms in your area or you'll come across a few healthy recipes on Pinterest that sound amazing.

If you imagine a loving, supportive marriage, you're letting your RAS know about its priority. Before you know it, you find that you're no longer attracted to the bad-influence girls who used to catch your eye, and you meet the woman of your dreams in line at the grocery store. Your RAS has learned who to look for.

If you create the mental image of a business that makes an impact on the world and on your bank account, your RAS is being put on notice about your important plans. Over time, ideas and concepts begin to flow through you, allowing you to bring your concept to life.

In this context, the Law of Attraction doesn't seem so mystical. We are not talking about folklore. This is science. The more you train your mind and let it know what things are important to you, the more you will begin to see evidence of the issues you have deemed essential to your life. You're not creating physical realities out of thin air. They were always there; your brain just wasn't giving them attention because it did not understand their importance. Once your RAS learns what you want to see (or become), the more it will open your attention—things will seem to appear from nowhere. But whatever it is was always there waiting for you to sense its presence.

You might be thinking that overhauling your filtration system and getting your RAS on board to create what you really want will be hard, especially if your mental patterns once gave pain and suffering top priority. Turning the cycle around seems intimidating. But if you embrace the habit of visualization and combine it with the awareness of your own RAS, you can begin to shift your brain's perspective of what you want to see as your life unfolds.

Pretty awesome, right? The old saying, "Be careful what you wish for because you just might get it" makes a lot more sense now, doesn't it? Your RAS is always trying to give you more of what you're summoning to your consciousness through your thoughts, beliefs, and words. The more you embrace this fact and harness the power of visualization, the more you will begin to notice what you desire showing up around you.

"I CAN'T EVEN IMAGINE DOING THAT!"

Have you ever let those words fly out of your mouth? Ever heard anyone else say them? I'm sure you have, but I want to make two important points here. One, you can absolutely imagine it. You have a mind that can dream up anything and everything. There are literally no limits to what your mind can visualize. Two, you will never be able to experience anything until you spend time imagining it. Whether it be running a marathon, moving away from home, or starting a business you're passionate about, you can't bring it to life until you've given your mind something to chew on. You have to embrace the powers of envisioning it first—then the action of bringing it to life can be initiated.

You must retrain your mind.

You must consciously take the reins and actively engage with positive visions, uplifting thoughts, and inspiring beliefs. This takes time, repetition, and faith. Once you start putting the mental work in, your RAS will kick on and assist. I am living proof! But you have to take the first little step toward your vision.

I wanted to show you what I do every day to bring my visions to life. I use daily "trigger time" to focus on my visualization and train my RAS. There are six times during the day that I stop and visualize my success:

- Morning: While I'm brushing my teeth, I use these three minutes to active my thoughts around my desires for the day.
- Car: When I get in my car to go to work, I sit quietly for three minutes and visualize my success.
- Gym: I start all my workouts with a little warmup cardio, and during the first three minutes before I start my audiobook, I visualize my success.
- Work: The first thing I do when I enter my studio or office is sit quietly for three minutes and visualize my success.
- Night: When I brush my teeth, I use these three minutes to visualize my success.
- Bed: This is my longest and most powerful visualization time of the day. The last thing I do before I go to sleep is create a video in my mind where I am doing all the things I desire.

Here's an example of what my bedtime visualization looks like:

My desire in authoring this book is to help people overcome their pain and live triumphant lives. So, I visualize countless thousands of people reading *The Purpose of Pain* followed by me speaking on a massive stage in front of the largest crowd you've ever seen.

My health and fitness are also at the forefront of my visualization process, so I always picture myself working out and looking super fit and healthy. I apply the same formula to my short-term and long-term goals. These “mental movie clips” of my desired future are constantly programming my RAS to respond in a positive way, allowing my mind to find opportunities destined to lead me to my goals.

Remember that everything that has ever been achieved or accomplished started with a vision; it’s all a matter of the mind first. Now, it’s time for you to get intentional with your visualization practice and use it as a powerful tool to create the opportunities you desire.

VISUALIZATION ACTION EXERCISE

Write down exactly what you desire. The items can be short-term or long-term goals; just write them down as clearly as possible.

Now, close your eyes and create a movie (complete with sights and sounds) of yourself doing exactly what you wrote down. This will help you cement the images in your brain and make it easier for you to use during your six daily visualizations.

Finally, create a checklist for each visualization session and mark them off daily as you complete them.

1. Morning __
2. Car __
3. Gym __
4. Work __
5. Night __
6. Bed __

I love the power of visualization. If I had to pick one of my practices as my favorite… Who am I kidding? I couldn't pick one. That would be like asking you to choose your favorite child. Yes, you probably have one, but you're not going to admit it.

The beauty of visualization is that you can literally do it anywhere and at any time. And the more you do it, the more powerful it becomes.

And much like the reframing exercise I shared with you earlier, it becomes second nature. I find myself visualizing my dreams and goals without even having to think about it.

Your mind can be your greatest enemy or your strongest ally, depending on how you decide to use it.

CHAPTER 20

HABITS, RITUALS, AND ROUTINES... THEY ALL MATTER

How you do one thing is how you do everything.

I'm sure you've heard some variation of this sentiment. I know people who believe it wholeheartedly and others who don't. I'm not here to pick a side in the debate; instead, I offer up my experience to help you understand the importance of the systems I share in this chapter. At this point, I've given you all the concepts, mindset shifts, and actions that have helped me find a true purpose from my pain. The information will prove most valuable to you if you have a structured system to bring it to life and reap all of the benefits.

When I'm thriving in all areas of life, and momentum is flowing in the right direction, everything is easier, more fulfilling, and downright amazing. Those times usually coincide with the days, weeks, and months that I'm showing up to embrace the work I've laid out for you in previous chapters. When I'm engaging with mindfultation, visualization, and taking notes from my Circle of Success, everything just flows. And it's fun.

I also know the opposite to be true. When I'm out of alignment and have put off the practices we've talked about, I feel off-center. When one area of my life is limping along, the other areas of my life seem to take a hit as well.

So, is it true that how you do one thing is how you do everything? Not necessarily. But when you're consistently showing up for yourself, the Universe tends to honor your commitment and make the day-to-day run a little more smoothly.

With that in mind, I do my best to optimize all the major areas of my life so nothing drags behind the others. These major areas are Health/Fitness, Relationships, Money, and Spirituality.

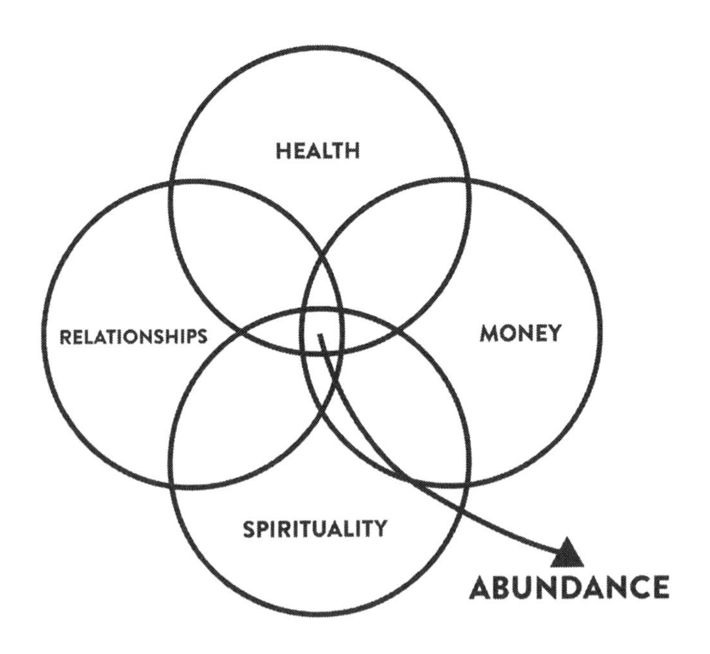

When all four of them are working in unison, I find myself in the middle of the Venn diagram shown above: living abundantly and enjoying it every step of the way. I'm a firm believer that we are nothing more than the sum of our habits, so to make sure I find my way to the middle of the diagram, I have systems in place to ensure that I am following the habits most likely to get me there. And I employ a weekly practice—my Sunday R.P.I. (more on this later)—to keep things in check every week.

Now that we've gotten to know each other and I know you're ready to embrace the process, I want to share my routines with you. If you wake up every morning and make time for the system I lay out, I promise everything in your life will begin to move forward.

MY MORNING RITUAL

"Holy Shit, I'm Alive!"

I know it's a bit dramatic, but these are actually the first words out of my mouth every morning. I started doing this a few years ago as a way to begin my day with extreme gratitude. Being alive is the greatest gift we have, and none of us celebrate it enough. So, I kick things off with a big celebration of being alive.

Gratitude

My next step is to get my journal out and write down a minimum of three things I'm grateful for in my life. Some mornings I write twenty and others just the three. There is no perfect number, but the act of gratitude starts your day on the right foot and your brain on the right focus. A grateful mind is a growing mind. Remember our little friend, the Reticular Activating System? This is also a great way to set the filters for what you want to experience and be aware of in your life. Setting your intention before your day begins is crucial.

Here's an example of my morning gratitude:

> *Today I am grateful for my amazing family—my life with Lori and Rudy is abundant and fulfilling.*

Today I am grateful for the opportunity to have a positive influence in the life of someone who needs an uplifting message or simply a word of encouragement.

Today I am thankful for cold brew coffee. (Yep, there are several days that coffee makes the top-three list in my journal. You see, your "gratefuls" don't have to be grandiose.)

Intention

Following my gratitude, I write down my intention for the day. My intention is how I am going to show up in the world. It's my declaration to the Universe of the man I will be that day.

Here's an example of my daily intention:

Today I will leave every person, place, and thing better than how I found it. I will lead with love and light in all of my encounters. I will shine the brightest in the darkest hours, and I will be the rock for those who seek a better way. I will hold place and space for those in need of help. Today I will be the change I seek in the world.

Actions

This is an important one because, as we now know, motion creates emotion, and the actions we take will help us to ride the momentum we've created.

I write down three actions I *will* take today that move me closer to the big goals or, as I call them, my *musts*. Now, these aren't suggestions or maybes, these are actions that I *must* get done.

Here are some example action steps you might take toward a big goal:

Big Goal Example #1: Lose 50 pounds in the next 90 days.

Action Step: Today I will only eat the foods I have prepared because I know that to achieve my goal of losing 50 pounds, it is essential to fuel my body with nutritious, healthy foods.

Action Step: Today I will go to the gym before work (6:00 a.m.) and do a minimum of 30 minutes of cardio and 15 minutes of legs. (Notice how specific I am with the time and movements. I didn't just say 15 minutes of weights. This detail eliminates any decision paralysis once you enter the gym and assures you will complete the action step.)

Action Step: Today I will stay out of the break room at work because I know it is filled with unhealthy foods that will not serve me on my quest to lose 50 pounds.

Big Goal Example #2: Plan a getaway with my partner in the next 90 days.

Action Step: Today I will shop around for locations we would enjoy, so I can determine how much money we're looking to invest in this trip.

Action Step: Today I will look at how much money we have and create a budget that will allow us to save for our vacation.

Action Step: Today I will make a list of everywhere we can cut spending to free up money for a more fulfilling experience.

Notice how I broke down the goals into 90-day outcomes. This is the perfect amount of time to use for goal achievement because it's long enough to conquer some big objectives and short enough that you don't lose focus.

Encouragements

My morning routine isn't just about setting the day up for success. It's also about supporting and encouraging those in my life to do the same.

Every morning I send a note of encouragement to three people in my life.

At this point, I write down the names of the people who will get a note from me that day. I don't send them right away for a couple of reasons:

I get up at 3:30 a.m. (it is not required to get up before dawn to make this process successful), and I know that most people are still asleep. As much as I'd love for my note of encouragement to be their wake-up call, I restrain myself out of respect.

Also, my phone and computer are on lockdown—you'll learn why in a minute.

This goes back to the African proverb, *If you want to go fast, go alone, but if you want to go far, go together.* When the people in my life win, I win, too. We are all connected; the more I encourage and support their journey, the more my journey is supported. I send these notes in various ways—text message, voice note, emails, and handwritten notes when that's an option. You are going to be blown away at the ripple effect of awesomeness this creates in your world and the world of the person receiving the note.

Here's an example of a note of encouragement I would send:

"Tommy, I'm proud of you, brother, and blessed to call you a friend. The impact you are making on the world is amazing. Have an awesome day and know I'm thinking about you."

Meditation/Mindfultation

Revisit the chapter on mindfultation to take some notes on the process and consider how you can use it for yourself.

Notice that everything to this point of the day is me dictating to the day and not the other way around. I don't check social media, emails, voicemails, or texts until after I've completed my morning routine. No exceptions.

My suggestion to you is to begin every morning with your phone either on airplane mode or, better yet, completely off. The same goes for the computer; do not open the lid until your morning routine is complete. If you start your day by responding to everyone else's needs, you will never take care of your own. Cut off your communication to start the day and come back to it after you've taken care of yourself. The emails, the texts, and the social media posts will be there after your morning routine. I promise.

Workout

Now, it's go time. The last part of my morning routine is movement. I personally go to the gym for an hour of cardio and weight lifting. It's my Zen happy time that primes me for a day of perfection. Your movement might be exactly like mine or it might be a walk, yoga, tennis, or even golf. The activity itself isn't an important piece of the process. As long as it brings you joy and gets your body physically moving, it's a win.

Time to take some action! Use the outline below to design your morning routine.

Gratitude

Write at least three things you are grateful for in your life.

1. ______________________________

2. ______________________________

3. ______________________________

Intention

Write your intention for today. How will you show up today?

____

____

____

____

____

____

Actions

Write three actions you *will* take today that move you closer to one of the big goals in your life. Remember, your big goals will fall into one of four circles: Health/Fitness, Relationships, Work/Money, Spirituality.

1. ______________________________

____

2. ______________________________

____

3. ______________________________

____

Encouragements

Write the names of three people you will send an encouraging note to this morning. Go ahead and use the space below to practice writing the note you'd send to the person you named.

Person #1: ____

Note: ____

____

____

____

Person #2: ____

Note: ____

____

____

____

Person #3: ______________________________

Note: ______________________________

____

____

____

Mindfultation

1. The "Brain Dump." Write down all the things currently floating around in your thoughts. Remember, don't judge, just write.

____

____

____

____

2. Make a mental note of all the nuggets or thoughts you need to get more clarity around. I've given you some space here to write because when you first begin this practice, you might need to rewrite or make notes on the *big* thoughts.

3. Now it's time to sit quietly with those thoughts. Be open to receive, and let your mind guide you to the clarity and answers. Use doodling to get even deeper into your subconscious mind.

4. It's journal time again. Write down anything that came to you during your quiet time of mindfulness. Don't judge your thoughts. Sometimes they won't make sense initially but the next day, or in a few hours, an aha moment will hit you like a ton of bricks. Reminder: You must be open to receive. If you don't believe, you can't receive.

Workout

Write your plan of action for your movement session today.

SUNDAY R.P.I.

Every Sunday I spend anywhere from an hour to a few hours on my R.P.I.

Here is the basis of the Sunday R.P.I.:

R: Reflection

Think about the past week. Write down your wins and strategically evaluate your challenges. Celebrate the things you did well and think deeply about some of the obstacles that came your way. Why were they a good thing? What did you learn from them? This is not an exercise of judgment, but one of clarity. Give yourself the gift of reflecting on what's going well and what could use adjusting.

P: Preparation

Get yourself mentally and physically prepared for the week ahead. What are the big rocks you will flip over this week? What are your action steps for the week ahead? This also includes your food, menu, and meal prep.

I: Intention

What is your intention for the upcoming week? Setting a strong intention for how your week *will* go is the foundation for achievement and progress. There are no coincidences—you are the result of your actions and decisions. Be intentional with them both.

There you have it! Now you have access to all of my systems. These have brought success to me and to thousands of clients who have personally worked with me. If you give attention and intention to everything listed here, I promise you will skyrocket your life to a level you haven't imagined.

Now you have all the tools to transform the pain of your past into a passion-led purpose. But before we close up shop here, I want to give you one last thing: permission.

EPILOGUE
PERMISSION SLIP

You've been seeking permission. You've been waiting for someone to tell you it's okay to step away from the memories of your pain and into the possibility that could come from transforming pain into something more meaningful. You're wired to wait for permission.

We spend every waking moment of our childhood waiting for someone to tell us what to do or give us the okay if we want to go somewhere. It's been so deeply baked into our DNA that most adults have a hard time shaking it off. We keep waiting for someone else—anyone besides our mature and capable selves—to tell us to move forward. We all want the nudge. We want a stamp of approval allowing us to go safely on our merry way toward the life we actually want to live.

Consider this your permission slip. You have the ultimate power of permission, but if you're looking for someone to hand it to you on a silver platter, it would be my pleasure.

In truth, you don't need anyone's approval except your own. You have to make the conscious decision that you want more for your life. You must decide it's okay to step forward even if it scares you half to death. Permission begins and ends with you. So, make the decision today. Here are some reminders of the gifts you should grant yourself:

Permission to move forward. This doesn't mean your past never happened or that you aren't accepting and acknowledging it. It means you're allowing yourself the option to move past it and to use the information as a catalyst for your growth instead of an anchor to your pain.

Give yourself permission to be imperfect. For many of us, our pain created the idea we had to be perfect to prevent the tragedy of the past from repeating. We now know this is simply not true. Moving forward will be messy; growth is never linear or without imperfection. Don't allow a false belief in perfectionism (either as an option or a possibility) to keep you stuck any longer.

Permission to figure it out as you go. A life lived in pain will keep you stuck in the idea that you must have all the answers before the journey can begin. This goes back to the desire to control every situation, believing that uncertainty is where bad things happen. Now that you know this is not true, allow yourself the grace to move forward without having all the answers or points plotted on your map ahead of time.

Permission to feel. This includes the pain. It's okay to feel the pain because now you understand it no longer has control over you. You can see now that pain is a driving force for your new story—not the stopping place it used to be. This also includes happiness and joy. Allowing yourself to feel these magic feelings doesn't mean you've forgotten or abandoned the past; it simply means you are no longer allowing it to control your life in a negative way.

Permission to choose. For so long, you've allowed other people and situations to make your choices for you. A newfound ability and desire to choose your new life's path is going to allow those feelings we just talked about. Embrace them, acknowledge them, and use them as fuel for your new story.

Permission to grow. You aren't stuck anymore. You aren't controlled anymore. You have to give yourself permission to grow through your pain and use it as a launching pad for your new life. You are who you are today because of your past pain; when you begin to see that, you will have a superpower to guide you for the rest of your life.

Giving yourself these permissions will be one of the greatest gifts you could ever receive because they will equip you to begin your new journey with the freedom you desire and deserve.

If you're brave enough to say goodbye, life will reward you with a new hello.[15]

~ Paulo Coelho

TO MAKE YOUR NEXT STEP EASIER...

You now have the information, tools, and examples to guide you through the process of writing your new story and turning your pain into purpose.

But as you know, there is more to it than just having the information and tools. And there's a big difference between being stuck in the Personal Development Vortex and acting on your new life without letting pain sit in the driver's seat.

A successful transition from pain to purpose will require you to show up every day as an active participant in your new story. Setting yourself up for success and creating this shift from old to new can and will only happen when you do the work required to keep you moving forward.

This is why I've created the next step of the process.

I've developed a six-week online workshop where I will guide you through the phases and process of creating your new story. The workshop will be delivered via video directly

15 Paulo Coelho (@paulocoelho), Twitter, April 18, 2012, https://twitter.com/paulocoelho/status/192573337921269760?lang=en.

to your inbox every week. There will be video training along with action steps for advanced work in moving past your pain and into your new purpose-filled life.

I'm excited to guide you through the process of turning your pain into purpose.

Go to

www.thepurposeofpain.com

for all the details.

Here's to your health, wealth, happiness, and newfound purpose.

Jay

ABOUT THE AUTHOR

Jay Nixon is a speaker, author, mentor, and coach whose mission is to help each and every person achieve their "absolute best self." He is the owner of the Thrive Fitness Studio in Palm Desert, California, and the creator of the Thrive Forever Fit Transformation Program, a personal development program designed to help you live your best life, found at www.ThriveForeverFit.com.

For over two decades, Jay has helped thousands of people achieve total body transformation through a cohesive combination of fitness, nutrition, and personal development coaching. Jay believes, "If you give people the right tools, education, and support, they can far surpass what they once thought was their maximum potential." He's known for his innate ability to get inside someone's head and help him/her achieve life-changing results.

Recognized as a lululemon Ambassador and dubbed by CBS News as "one of the best fitness and nutrition experts in the business," Jay has been featured on ABC and FOX and in *Health Magazine* and *Triathlete Magazine*. When he's not working with clients one-on-one, you'll find him consulting for Fortune 1000 companies in the nutrition and fitness industry.

Jay is the author of the Amazon best-selling book *The Overweight Mind: The Undeniable Truth Behind Why You're Not Losing Weight,* also found at www.TheOverweightMind.com.

REFERENCES

Brett, Regina. "Regina Brett's 45 Life Lessons and 5 to Grow On." *Cleveland Plain Dealer* (May 28, 2006), https://www.cleveland.com/brett/blog/2006/05/regina_bretts_45_life_lessons.html

Brockway, Rev Laurie Sue. "31 Motivational Quotes from Dr. Wayne Dyer," *Huffington Post*, updated December 7, 2017, https://www.huffpost.com/entry/-wayne-dyer_b_8066286.

Brown, Sunni. *The Doodle Revolution: Unlock the Power to Think Differently.* New York: Portfolio – Penguin, 2014.

Byrne, Rhonda, dir. *The Secret.* Prime Time Productions, 2006.

Dyer, Wayne. *Manifesting Your Destiny: The Nine Spiritual Principles for Getting Everything You Want.* New York: HarperCollins, 1997.

Jha, Alok. "Where belief is born." *The Guardian.* June 30, 2005. https://www.theguardian.com/science/2005/jun/30/psychology.neuroscience.

Hay, Louise L. *You Can Heal Your Life Gift*. Carlsbad, CA: Hay House, Inc., 1999.

MindBodyGreen. n.d. “Gandhi: Your Beliefs Lead to Your Destiny.” https://www.mindbodygreen.com/0-2957/Gandhi-Your-Beliefs-Lead-to-Your-Destiny.html

Murakami, Haruki. *What I Talk about when I Talk about Running: A Memoir* (New York: Vintage Books, 2008).

Pressfield, Steven. *The War of Art*. Self-published, 2012.

Robbins, Tony. *Awaken The Giant Within*. New York: Simon and Schuster, 2012.

Made in the USA
Columbia, SC
23 October 2023